AA-NOT THE ON[...]
2nd Edition

D0621875

YOUR ONE STOP RESOL[...]
TO 12-STEP ALTERNATIVES
INCLUDING A COMPREHENSIVE DIRECTORY
OF LICENSED PROFESSIONALS AND
TREATMENT PROGRAMS

"Some books get better and better with each passing edition. This is the case of "AA Not The Only Way", written by Melanie Solomon…Overall, this is a book whose existence needs to be shouted from the rooftop, evangelized on street corners, and should be REQUIRED READING in EVERY Alcohol and Drug Counselor certification program in the United States! A copy should be sent to every drug and alcohol treatment center in the U.S., and most importantly, this book should ON THE DESK OF EVERY "coercing authority" that has the power to "force" people with addictive disorders, into treatment facilities… If you are in recovery, or know someone who is, or wants to be, this book is a MUST READ! Don't start or continue a recovery path without it!"
John McCready, NCAC-I, M-RAS
Oceanside, CA

"As a dedicated member of a 12 Step recovery program one may think that my review on Melanie's book "AA Not the Only Way" might be one of disapproval. However you would be mistaken.
AA Not the Only Way pulls no punches when describing Melanie's personal experience with conventional treatment and 12 Step fellowships. Determined to tell her story truthfully it may appear to be a bashing of these programs, but in reality nothing could be further from the truth.
Having said that may I say that this book is an absolute must read for anyone seeking an alternative to conventional treatment, 12 Step fellowships and typical court ordered solutions of the day… this book is as important to the recovery community as any other method available today. The simple truth is Melanie Solomon's book has successfully convinced KHLT Recovery Radio and myself that her book is a must read for all in recovery. !2 Step or otherwise. Thank You Melanie for a Job Very Well Done."
Monty Meyer
Executive Producer
KHLT Recovery Radio

MELANIE SOLOMON

FOREWORD BY MARC F. KERN, PH.D.

PREFACE BY FREDERICK ROTGERS, PSY.D.

Published by Capalo Press

www.capalo.com

3705 Arctic PMB 2571

Anchorage, Alaska   99503

http://www.aanottheonlyway.com

aanottheonlyway@gmail.com

AA-Not the Only Way; Your One Stop Resource Guide to 12-Step Alternatives:
Including a Comprehensive Directory of Licensed Professionals and Treatment
Programs/ Melanie Solomon; foreword by Dr. Marc F. Kern; preface by Dr.
Frederick Rotgers; edited by Ana Hayes and Lynn "Kayla" Baugh.

Includes bibliographical references.

ISBN# 978-0-9762479-9-9

TABLE OF CONTENTS

FOREWORD

Dear friends,

I have long awaited this directory of addiction treatment alternatives. It represents what I believe to be the future of the field. It is a pioneering effort to organize this unique body of knowledge. A directory of this type was never available before -- in part due to technology, but also because there were so few providers of non-12-step based services.

As you can see, the field is growing and maturing. In no way is this directory bashing AA or saying that the 12-step method is wrong. Rather, it is the first project to document that there is a real need for alternatives, because as we all know one size of anything is not right for everyone.

Scientific research has been showing that the traditional AA approach only retains about 5% of those who walk through their doors. Apparently, not a very attractive mythology for 21st century consumers to achieve sobriety. While other more contemporary methods, including motivational therapy, cognitive therapy and brief interventions are proving to be much more effective.

As a pioneer in this field myself, this document represents a significant endorsement of what I have always believed in since I sought help for my addictions: that people want new ways to talk, think and resolve their addictions, or just manage their life better. A new way that is not clouded by traditional verbiage and notions about the phenomenon we call addiction.

The programs and resources listed here are out of the 12-step box. Their effectiveness has yet to be fully tested, but they represent a new hope, a new type of solution for those suffering from addiction. I believe the future of healthcare depends on opening up one's eyes to the realities of a world where chemical substances can be helpful as well as harmful. A new world where there is much more personal choice for one's lifestyle; where people's needs and wants direct the treatment of harmful behavior -- not the other way around.

This directory is a result of months of research in the field of addiction, and for anyone with a problem with drugs or alcohol, provides valuable information about the growing number of options available to achieve a happy and healthy life.

Bravo Melanie.

Marc F. Kern Ph.D.

http://www.aa2.org

http://www.HabitDoc.com

http://www.addictioninfo.org

http://www.addictionalternatives.com

PREFACE

In 1991 the National Clearinghouse on Alcohol and Drug Information published a poster with the title "Typical American Alcoholic". The intent of the poster was to inform the general public about the incredible diversity among people with alcohol (and by implication) drug-related problems. Sixteen portraits are presented in the poster, showing both men and women, as well as people with different skin coloring, and clearly different dress. The point being that there is no such thing as a "typical" person with alcohol or drug problems. If this message is in fact true, and I believe it is, then why is it that for more than four decades we have insisted that the same basic approaches be used for every single person who comes in contact with a treatment program or provider for help with an alcohol or drug-related problem?

Since the 1940s, when Marty Mann, the first women to become sober in Alcoholics Anonymous, formed that National Council on Alcoholism (NCA, later the National Council on Alcoholism and Drug Dependence, NCADD) with the express purpose of de-stigmatizing alcoholism (and later other drug dependence) by promoting the notion that alcoholism was a medical "disease", NCADD and numerous other public and private organizations (including the National Institute on Drug Abuse, whose former head, Dr. Alan Leshner declared with absolute certainty "addiction is a brain disease.") have joined in that effort. It is safe to say that, at least in the United States, the "disease" notion of addiction has become the most widely accepted view of addiction, both by the general public and by many treatment providers.

In medicine, diseases are often complex phenomena, varying in severity from individual to individual, sometimes varying in course, and often requiring different treatments depending on the particular patient and his/her biological circumstances. In medicine when treating chronic relapsing diseases (such as diabetes, hypertension, or asthma) physicians utilize a wide variety of medications and behavioral approaches that are frequently tailored to fit the particular patient. For example, a recent Google search retrieved information showing that there are at least seven classes of medication used to treat hypertension, and within each class there are six to eight specific medications available. This search did not include formulations that combine one or more medications. Simple arithmetic suggests, therefore, that there are at least 50 different medication approaches to treating hypertension. This does not include a variety of behavioral strategies (dietary changes, increasing exercise, etc.) that are typically part of treatment for this chronic disease.

All of this is to point out a basic conundrum in how we address helping people with alcohol or drug-related problems. Why is it that despite the widespread insistence that such problems are nearly as diverse as the people who suffer from them, and the widely held belief that these problems are the result of a "disease", much like the chronic diseases I have just mentioned, we have for decades maintained that there is virtually only <u>one</u> appropriate treatment for people with alcohol or drug problems—confrontational (if necessary) referral to 12-step based support groups coupled with counseling

4

aimed at convincing the patient that he/she suffers from a "disease" that requires lifelong abstinence from all psychoactive substances in order for the "disease" to be arrested (but never "cured").

This notion, that "one size fits all" in the treatment of alcohol and drug problems has been thoroughly debunked by scientific research. In fact, as long ago as 1990, the Institute of Medicine asserted that there is no one universally effective treatment for alcohol or drug problems. Yet, we have persisted in sending our children, our spouses, our partners, our employees, and even our criminals to the same, single mode of treatment. And we then wonder why only a small percentage of the people we attempt to fit into the 12-step cubby hole, get better. And, we have done this despite the fact that there are a variety of other psychological and pharmacological treatments that have been shown by solid scientific research to be highly successful in helping people with alcohol or drug problems, even when our cherished traditional approaches have been either resistant to scientific study or have not shown up well when rigorous research has compared them to the alternative treatments, many of which have been around for 3 decades or more!

As consumers, I suspect you wonder why it is that treatment providers have not "jumped on the band wagon" to learn and employ these new evidence-based approaches to treatment. There are many reasons for this failure to grow on the part of treatment providers, but I will not rehearse them here. Suffice it to say that there are alternatives to the traditional 12-step oriented, often confrontational approaches that have been virtually the only treatment available in the United States. The problem is finding treatment providers who provide these alternative, evidence-based approaches. Melanie Solomon has taken a wonderful step toward making that process, of identifying alternatives to traditional treatments, easier. By both providing her own story as a justification for this book, and by listing an ever growing list of providers who use up-to-date, evidence-based approaches in their work helping people with alcohol and drug problems, Ms. Solomon has done a great public service.

Her work is not finished, however, with the publication of this directory of alternative resources. Daily more and more treatment programs and providers begin to receive training in these new, effective approaches to working with people who have alcohol and drug problems. For now, though, this is an excellent starting point for patients, their families and those who are close to them who wish to find help that does not emphasize "powerlessness", but rather empowers consumers to find the most effective help for alcohol and drug problems.

Frederick Rotgers, PsyD, ABPP
Associate Professor of Psychology
Philadelphia College of Osteopathic Medicine

MY STORY

When I woke up, I found myself on my living room floor. I couldn't remember anything, but I knew that something was terribly wrong. When I made it to the bathroom and pulled myself up to look in the mirror, I was shocked at what I saw. I did not recognize the reflection staring back at me. I was covered in blood, one eye was black and swollen to almost twice its normal size, I had several bumps on my head, and my body was covered in bruises. I didn't know what had happened. I wondered if I had a seizure and had blacked out. I began to shake. I was scared, uncertain, disoriented…

10 Years Earlier…

Having been accepted by UCLA Law School, it looked like all those years of endless studying had finally paid off. I was 22 and my life was full of promise. I was going to become a lawyer, just like my dad. My life was going to be perfect, or so I thought. Sure I partied and experimented with drugs in high school and college, but it never interfered with my schooling or anything else. The only close call had been when my boyfriend turned me on to cocaine during a semester off one year in college. But after a few months of doing it, I realized that I would have to snort cocaine all the time, 24/7, or not at all because I loved the high but couldn't stand coming down. So, I quit.

The summer I was accepted into law school, I went to see a doctor about my migraines and he prescribed for me a nasal spray that I had never heard of. It seemed like a good solution; one I had no apparent reason to question but should have because before the end of the week, I was hooked. (Later when I researched the medication I found out it was not just a nose spray, but actually a form of liquid morphine). Using this prescription set off a chain of events during my first year of law school that would eventually lead to my demise. After my prescription ended and my headache specialist in Los Angeles would not prescribe anything stronger than Imitrex, I began taking Vicodin. I had never abused Vicodin before, but when I ran out of that nasal spray, I began to feel violently ill. In order to make it through the day or even function, I had to have something in my system. Unfamiliar with addiction at that time, I had no idea what I was suffering from was withdrawal symptoms. All I had done was take some medication my doctor had prescribed to me. He had never once warned me about the possibility of becoming addicted to it.

During this time, I began experiencing extreme anxiety and panic attacks, so I went to see a psychiatrist who immediately put me on benzodiazapams, which are more commonly known as benzos. I was prescribed Xanax and valium for my anxiety, induced by the withdrawal from the nasal spray, as well as Ativan for sleep. By the end of the year, I had built up a tolerance not only to pain pills but Benzos as well.

Upon trying to quit taking the pills, I was horrified to find out that I could not stop. By the beginning of my second year of law school, I was a mess, both

6

physically and emotionally. After sharing my predicament with my mother, a therapist, and my father, a lawyer who is also a strong advocate of AA, I was admitted to an alcoholic rehabilitation center. This is where I was introduced first hand to Alcoholics Anonymous, commonly referred to as AA, and its sister programs, Narcotics Anonymous, NA, and Cocaine Anonymous, CA. I was also introduced to the whole "incurable and progressive disease" concept, which was grilled into me as the one and only undeniable cure. I was never told that there were any other solutions or treatments in existence.

And so began my Nine-year nightmare, where my life ceased to be my own, where I was told to stop thinking for myself, because "it was my best thinking that had gotten me here in the first place," and that my intelligence was actually blamed as my roadblock to staying sober.

But staying sober wasn't my problem. The pills were my problem and I was very clear with the rehab people regarding the help I needed. I needed help getting off the pills so I could get back to my life. Knowing this to be true, I brought my law books and laptop with me so I wouldn't fall behind in my studies. However, the staff refused to listen and continually insisted I was an alcoholic and took my laptop and studies away. My boyfriend came to advocate for me and they refused to listen to him as well. I pleaded with them that I had never been addicted to alcohol or any other drug in my life until now. I showed them the warning labels on the prescription pills, which stated they might be habit forming and addictive. They laughed, patted me on the head and said, "Don't worry, honey. You just don't know it yet, but by the end of your stay here, you'll realize that you're one of us, that you are an alcoholic. Right now you're in *denial*."

So I attended the required AA meetings, 90 meetings in 90 days, and found what they were saying to be true: "Go to enough meetings and you'll end up just catching alcoholism!" This might sound ridiculous, but this is exactly what happened. I caught alcoholism! Stating, "I'm Melanie and I'm an alcoholic" over and over, sometimes twenty times a day, was not only a negative affirmation, but I began to internalize it as well. Before I knew it, I had created this entire story surrounding the fact that I was a victim of this incurable, progressive, fatal disease called alcoholism, and that there was no way out.

As most people, I was vulnerable entering rehab. I was lost, confused and I started believing what the "professionals" were telling me. (I now know that most "professionals" at traditional rehabs are merely drug and alcohol counselors who have had some "clean time" in a 12-step program). At the end of my 30 days, my counselors told me I needed to go into their sober living program and I complied since I still needed their help and my dad's financial assistance. So I listened to him and did whatever they told me to do. My life just got worse with frightening speed. I was told that anyone who was not an alcoholic or an addict would not be able to understand me. My boyfriend, the love of my life, was not an addict. He was what they called a "normie", so I broke up with him because I believed that he couldn't possibly understand me anymore or what I was going through. Soon, law school became too stressful and began to interfere with my "recovery" and all of the AA meetings I had to attend, so I quit. I couldn't hold down a job anymore, so I decided I had to go on disability, because I was not well and had this incurable disease called alcoholism that was "trying to kill me on a daily basis". I was now officially on the recovery merry-go-round. Staying sober in the program for 6 months to a year, I would eventually relapse, ending up in a rehab or hospital emergency room, or sometimes even a psych ward. This had become my life!

This insanity continued for nine long years. I spent all of my time trying to get and stay sober with the use of a 12-step program, which I had been told by countless rehabs, doctors and other 12-step members was "the only way" out. With each relapse, I ended up feeling more and more hopeless, thinking towards the end that I must be one of those people that the *Big Book of Alcoholics Anonymous* talks about as being "constitutionally incapable of being honest with themselves". My life was becoming more and more meaningless. Even while sober, my life revolved around working the steps and going to meetings and relapsing again and again. And again.

With each relapse, I became less and less confident in myself, to the point that even with six months sober, I decided to put myself into a sober living facility and stay there for over a year because I had lost all faith and trust in myself that I could stay sober living on my own. That became my sole focus in life. Nothing else mattered except that I stay clean and sober. I no longer knew who I was, except that I was an "alcoholic" and an "addict." I had completely lost myself. I no longer knew who I was. I had lost touch with my friends and family. I had left my life, my home and my animals behind. My family lost respect for me, thinking that once again I had failed the program and that there must be something terribly wrong with me. I was caught in my own personal hell that I thought would never end. I did not think I would ever see the light again. I was caught in a vicious cycle of institutions, rehabs, sober livings, AA meetings, relapsing, and ending up back in rehab, *again*. This cycle fits perfectly under AA's own definition of insanity: "To do the same thing over and over again, expecting different results." In fact, I'll just quote James DeSenna's definition of insanity:

Insanity: 12-step addiction treatment and lifelong "recovery," that is, doing the same thing over and over while expecting different results,   despite its lack of efficacy and obvious negative, and sometimes deadly, consequences." (DeSena, *Overcoming Your Alcohol, Drug and Recovery Habits, 2003).*

After 10 years of hell… I woke up on the living room floor, covered in blood; I was horrified by what I saw…

I had just returned home from my Saturday meeting. I had recently put my cat, Felix, to sleep, the week before, and I was completely devastated. I really felt like having a few glasses of wine, but I knew if I drank, this would mean yet another relapse. That would mean starting all over again; letting everyone down, especially my family, and I'd have to raise my hand as a newcomer, and "lose" all my time again. I couldn't handle that kind of shame, not even one more time.

So instead, I decided to try to get a harmless buzz from an old prescription I still had. I took a few more pills than I normally would have, but what I took reacted horribly with the antidepressants that I was taking. I apparently had a major overdose, as well as multiple seizures, ultimately giving myself a concussion.

When I came to on the living room floor, I was horrified by what I saw. I had lost all control of my bodily functions. Later I found out that this often occurs right before a person dies. But for some reason I did not die. When I looked over at the couch, one of the cushions was entirely covered in diarrhea which was also stuck in my hair and smeared all over my living room. I had almost died because I didn't want to have the "stigma" of an alcoholic relapse. Unlike many others on this recovery merry-go-round who when thrown off their horse have landed in death, I was one of the lucky ones.

After a few days of recuperation, crying and praying, it suddenly came to me that there had to be another way, even though during my nine years in AA no one had ever told me that there was. Awakened and filled with hope, curiosity and purpose, for the first time in my life, it became crystal clear that AA was not only *not* working for me, but had become detrimental to my life. I got on the internet and began furiously searching for alternatives to AA. I was driven and began researching and working around the clock as though not only my life depended on it, but the lives of countless others who shared similar experiences. To my amazement I found that there were many wonderful options to AA, and I wasn't the only one out there for whom AA had failed. I soon realized that I had not failed the program. It just wasn't for me. In fact, it doesn't work for most people! The more research I did, the more driven and astonished I became. Why was I never told about any of the other options that were readily available? None of the rehabs, institutions, counselors, sponsors, therapists, doctors, *nobody* had told me that there were viable alternatives, ones that were proving to be more effective than AA! I knew that I had to get this information not only for myself but for others experiencing the hopelessness and despair that I had felt. This book provides a multitude of other solutions that are available in addition to or instead of AA. What you are about to read will astonish you at first, but it will open you up to new possibilities leaving you with hope, a word that too many of us have forgotten the meaning of. My prayers are that this book will help you find it once again.

I am now 33 years old, and have never felt so free in my life. While we are all on this life's journey together, we are all unique. It is my great desire that we can all find solutions that work for us as individuals. There are many different paths. The most important thing I've learned is that there are more than one, and what works for one person, might not work for another. All that matters now is that a door has been opened for us to see that there *are* alternatives, and we have choices! With the information I have found, you can now make an informed decision for a treatment program that feels right for you or a loved one. My nine heartbreaking years of trying the same program over and over again expecting different results was an experience I went through out of ignorance; both my own and the recovery industry's as well. This is an experience I pray none of you have to go through, or if you've already been through it, you can use this information to stop the cycle right now. Knowledge is power. And AA is not the only way. Thank God.

With the updated version of this book, three years have passed since I wrote the above story…one year was fabulous, the next one my greatest downfall, and the latest my long struggle back. After writing this book, I felt great! I was finally getting an important message out by doing press releases, doing lectures and going on radio shows. I was working day and night and going to my kundalini yoga classes which, for me, worked better for my sobriety than any meeting I had ever gone to. Unfortunately, after about five months, I stopped going to yoga, and was not doing anything else that I wrote about in my book that could have also helped me. (You can have all the information in the world, but unless you apply it to your life, it won't help you!) Instead, I focused exclusively on my work, having absolutely no balance in my life. I was beginning to be stressed out all of the time. Plus, and most importantly, I had been misdiagnosed for years, as just having some anxiety and depression, when in reality, I was bipolar 2. Therefore, I was improperly medicated for my sensitive chemical imbalance.

At about the nine month mark, I had an actual physical breakdown, where my thyroid, adrenals and other crucial systems simply shut down. I had no energy, to the point where walking to the bathroom seemed to be too hard. While I was in this weakened state, my ex-boyfriend and best friend came to stay with me to help me out. He ended up bringing crack cocaine back to my house (which I had never done before) and I actually let him convince me that it would give me some of my energy back and let me get back to work. Well, it DID give me energy, but after a week of using cocaine, he went out and got heroin, his drug of choice, and overdosed on my couch. I thought he was just passed out for the night, but when he was in the same position the next day, I knew something was wrong. It turned out he was in a vegetative state and stayed that way for months until he was declared brain dead and the plug was pulled.

I LOST it after that. One minute we were getting back together, and the next he was DEAD! I mean, I've overdosed so many times, but I just come out of it…how could he not?? It just did not compute. I tried to focus again on my work but something inside me had snapped. A friend, who later became my boyfriend, came over to my house. He happened to be on a crack run at the time (which I didn't know about). He pulled some out and asked me if I wanted to smoke some. Since I didn't really care about my life anymore, I joined him, not thinking about any of the consequences because at this time I was welcoming death. We smoked crack day and night for about a month. I no longer cared about anything, not even my love of doing my life's work of helping people with their addictions and their suffering. I just couldn't care. Nothing was left in me. Between my physical health and then my mental, emotional and spiritual health, I was going down, and going down fast. I honestly think my cat was the only thing keeping me from completely doing myself in because she had no one else to care for her.

Before doing crack, I hadn't done cocaine in almost 15 years, and I stopped on my own because I realized it had the potential of becoming a problem. Crack was 100 times worse. I needed it all the time. I spent all of my money on it to the point of being broke and homeless. I had a crypt gang member crash in my front glass door because I owed him money, but I still didn't care. I did not care if I lived or died. Period. So even this event didn't scare me in the least.

Finally, we stopped using for a few months and tried to get some help, but eventually relapsed on New Years Eve. My life got even worse than I could ever imagine. My apartment, my safe haven, got completely trashed and I had to give it up. Everything I owned got destroyed and I was living in utter filth. My boyfriend got arrested for possession right outside my door. My website got taken down and all that I worked so hard for was going down the toilet. My lungs and ribs hurt so badly I could barely breathe. I later found out I had almost fatal pneumonia. Still, all I mainly cared about was getting and staying high. This went on for another month, until the morning I was having major oral surgery. I almost didn't wake up out of the general anesthesia and when I did, my life became pretty much a living hell. I wished I had just stayed asleep.

Since I had no more home to go back to, I stayed at my boyfriend's parents while he was at a sober living facility (my worst nightmare). The pain did not go away in my chest, so I went to the ER where I stayed for a whole month getting Demerol shots every four hours. After that, I had to go to into a hospital program to detox of all the meds I got in the hospital, then back to the parents' house to look for a good dual diagnosis program (since as I stated, I am bipolar 2 which is a whole other issue that needs to be addressed).

After doing much research, I found there are very few places that specialize in dual diagnosis and when I was confronted with a couple of very poor choices, I thought my only option was to die…to get out. I couldn't take the pain, stress and suffering anymore and it seemed like no one could really help me. My depression and anxiety were at an all time high. I took all the pills that I had on hand, which were a LOT since I've been on just about all of them trying to get the right mixture. I downed them with some alcohol, I wrote a note, smoked what I thought was going to be my last cigarette, and laid down. Well, my boyfriend's mom found me, didn't think anything was wrong until she found the note, and then called 911. I went to the hospital and they made me drink charcoal. My life was as bad as ever.

I have been diagnosed with Bipolar 2, which means I get simultaneous major depression along with high anxiety, PTSD, in addition to ADHD . Most treatment programs don't have the qualified staff or programs to address these conditions which are at least as important as the addiction itself. Research has shown that 70% of all people with substance abuse problems also have some co-occurring disorder, so why are programs not adapting to meet these needs? This is one reason so many people are falling through the cracks, relapsing, overdosing and killing themselves. People are almost guaranteed to fail if neither their addictions nor their co-occurring disorders are addressed.

Luckily, I did end up finding a good rehab program that could deal simultaneously with my addictions and co-occurring disorders. I was able to finally heal and recover from my boyfriend's death, get stable on my medications and learn how to get and maintain balance in my life. Things I have found helpful with regards to balance include using exercising, meditating, positive thinking and therapy. I have begun to realize happiness is a choice, so why not choose it? I have spent too many years living in misery. I have made the choice now to live differently. I am telling you that you too have that choice.

If people, including me, are going to have a chance at leading happy, successful and sober lives, it is all of the co-occurring issues that have to be dealt with and resolved. There are some who think that these co-occurring issues need to be addressed first, while others say it can happen simultaneously with addictions treatment. It can also depend on what the primary problem is. For example, if a person mainly has psych problems and it is only when their medications are out of balance or something else occurs that sets off their primary condition, then this needs to be handled before any real sobriety can take place. Otherwise, relapse is almost inevitable.

It took me a long time to accept that I was dually diagnosed. Now I finally have. I have no other choice. If I don't, I will continue on this horrible cycle and never get the help I need. When I "relapse", it's not to party or for any other reason. It's because I'm out of balance and am trying to self medicate with prescriptions, or other cocktails, the best that I know how. This cannot happen anymore because my last, best answer, was to simply take my own life. If I did this, there would be no way I could go on doing what I love, which is helping others get through life, just as I have, whatever their diagnosis or problem.

So many people need help and I would be honored to be one of those who understood from first hand knowledge, thereby being able to offer my experience, strength and hope and some real helpful direction for others who so desperately need it.

Even if AA works great in keeping someone sober, it doesn't address co-occurring issues, which is why the "Big Book of AA" encourages people to seek outside help. This is nothing to be ashamed of, since most of us have deep, underlying issues and drinking and using is a symptom of that. It is the root which needs to be discovered and dealt with and eventually discarded. Once that happens, the need to use mind altering substances will start to dissipate on its own.

No matter what path you decide to take to stop or moderate your drinking, it is dealing with your co-occurring (primary or secondary condition) which is going to allow you to sustain your health for good. We are all individuals, and there are just as many ways of coping with our struggles as there are our problems with alcohol or drugs. Please see future chapters that can address these issues, then pick and choose the ones that you feel will work for you. This will ultimately determine your success, and more! As for me, I am still finding my path. What has worked best in my life has been getting and staying on the right medications, doing yoga, meditating and daily affirmations. I know I am fortunate in my knowledge of all the options and resources out there to be with me on my journey. Now you will have that as well.

INTRODUCTION

"Keep coming back. It works if you work it!" This is what is chanted at the end of every meeting, but what if you *have* "worked it" and you still keep going back and getting drunk or loaded? Now, most people in the program will say things like, "Well, you must not have *really* done the steps right," or "You didn't go to *enough* meetings," or "You didn't pray to your Higher Power," or "You know you did *something wrong* or else you would still be sober!"

Since what you are taught to believe the minute you step into a 12-step Program is, "You either *get* AA, or you die," you tend to stop thinking for yourself, (since it was your "best thinking that got you here"), stop questioning, and just follow what other's tell you to do. This would be fine if this is what worked… but unfortunately, evidence is proving otherwise.

The 12-step success rate is showing to be approximately 3 percent. Yes, that's right… only 3 percent! (Brown, *Treatment Doesn't Work*, 1991). Here are some more startling statistics:

- 45% of the people who attend Alcoholics Anonymous meetings never return after their first meeting.
- 95% never return after the first year.
- 5% retention rate (Based on Alcoholics Anonymous World Services' own statistics).
- 93-97% of conventional drug rehabs and alcohol treatment centers are 12-step or AA based, so those who leave AA to look elsewhere, such as conventional alcohol and drug treatment for solutions, are essentially rejoining AA!

Let's look at these numbers in even *more* detail: For many years in the 1970s and 1980s, the AA GSO (Alcoholics Anonymous General Service Organization) conducted triennial surveys where they counted their members and asked questions like how long members had been sober. Around 1990, they published a commentary on the surveys: *Comments on A.A.'s Triennial Surveys* [no author listed, published by Alcoholics Anonymous World Services, Inc., New York, no date (probably 1990)]. The document has an AA identification number of "5M/12-90/TC". The document was produced for AA internal use only. Averaging the results from the five surveys from 1977 to 1989 yielded the following numbers:

- 81% attendees are gone (19% remain) after 1 month;
- 90% attendees are gone (10% remain) after 3 months,
- 93% attendees are gone (7% remain) after 6 months,
- And 95% are gone (5% remain) at the end of one year.

That gives AA a maximum possible success rate of only 5% (even if you define "success" as staying sober for *only* one year). That is not what a competent doctor would call good medical treatment. The FDA would never approve a medicine that is only successful on 5% of the patients. (Kolenda, Golden Text Publishing Company, 2003).

AA hardly sounds like a "proven method," let alone one that works for most people. So, if only about 5% of the people are getting the help that they need, what about the 95% of the people who are not being helped? *That* is the purpose of this booklet… to provide much needed information to individuals, rehabilitation centers, hospitals, sober living units, and even 12-step programs themselves so that people with substance abuse problems can be helped. The bottom line is this… is the goal to get alcoholics and addicts into AA or NA or CA, or is it to actually get them help?
Let me mention from the start that I think 12-step programs are wonderful for those individuals who it *does* work for. I have seen it change many lives for the better, including my dad's, who has now had 17 years of continuous sobriety, maintaining his sobriety from his very first meeting. It is also a great fellowship to share experiences, strength and hope. So, in *no* way am I anti-AA, however, it is becoming clearer to me that substance abuse is not a "one size fits all" problem., Let's look at how AA can help before pointing out some drawbacks.

AA has been helping alcoholics quit drinking since 1935. Current membership is in the millions so you can find meetings all day long, 7 days a week. AA offers social support based on a spiritual model. People help each other stay sober and gain guidance from each other. Each member also works through the "12 steps", giving the person a set of ethical and moral goals to achieve. It also offers total involvement in a sober community, which makes it easier for you to break away from your drinking and using. When you join AA, you join a ready-made social scene to replace the drug and alcohol scene. As an AA member, you can gain a sense of belonging, which can make you feel more valued yourself.

In a way, AA destigmatizes alcoholism. You're seen as a person with a disease so it's no your fault. However, you are responsible for your sobriety and staying sober. AA may help you accept that you even have a problem. Slogans are short, often clichéd statements, which tend to help people stay sober, and they actually are very similar to what you would learn in cognitive-behavioral therapy. (So you don't even have to like AA to utilize them.) The most well known is most likely, "*One day at a time.*" By using this slogan, you are not shaming yourself for your past, nor are you worrying about your future. You can stay in the moment and tell yourself, "If it's this bad tomorrow, I'll drink," and most of the time, people with years of sobriety say this never has to happen. This is a good, healthy exercise to practice, not only in regard to alcohol or drugs, but to everything in life. It keeps you from getting too overwhelmed and just giving up on whatever you are trying to accomplish. It also relieves much anxiety and fear, by enabling you to fully live in the present.

"*Think it through*" is another helpful slogan. When you find yourself thinking about how great it was when you were getting drunk or high, (this is called selective memory), think of all the consequences that follow that action, whether it's a huge hangover, drunk driving, getting arrested, whatever the negative consequences that usually happen to you. This can help you to stop "romanticizing" your drinking and using, getting you back to reality, which in turn will help you to avoid returning to it.

"*HALT*" (Don't get too Hungry, Angry, Lonely or Tired) is one you'll hear all the time and is also known in cognitive-behavioral therapy as "internal cues." It's interesting to note that most relapses occur due to emotional discomfort and wanting to self-medicate.

"*Take what you like and leave the rest*" basically says it all. Everything in the 12-step program are merely suggestions; they are not orders. So, if there are parts of the program or fellowship that you do not like or do not resonate with you, ignore them and just focus on the aspects that you might find helpful. And the program is free! So, if you've never been to AA, or another 12-step meeting, I would suggest trying a few and seeing if they are for you. If they are, then you might not have to look any further. If not, do not despair. There are many other alternatives that could work for you and for the 80% to 95% who are not "making it" in AA. So what are some of the 12-step programs' drawbacks?

There has been much scientific research done since the 1930's, and AA takes into account none of the relevant data; they never change, so many professionals have criticisms of AA, mainly:

AA ignores the physical. There is no medical advice given and no information on healing. You get no encouragement to change your diet, exercise, or learn stress reduction techniques (all very important to staying sober.) In fact, at most meetings you'll find doughnuts, coffee and cigarettes as the mainstay "diet". This can be the worst on your central nervous system and create more anxiety which is just a setup for an impending relapse.

AA requires social involvement. This is great unless you get nervous in groups and usually drink to get by in these types of social situations. AA requires some belief in God, or a "Higher Power". Six out of the 12 steps refer to God or some greater power so you'll be lost if you don't start to believe in something. Many people are put off by the religious thinking that dominates 12-step programs. These groups claim to be spiritual, and not religious. However, there is a clear Christian origin to many or their beliefs. The idea of being powerless, and the only answer being to 'turn your will and lives over to the care of God as you understand him" does not sit well with a lot of people. They want to have some power in reclaiming their lives. This is especially true for those who are not religious and for people who have traditionally been put into roles of being powerless their whole lives, such as women and minorities.

Many people have problems with the public confessional approach. At meetings, members constantly recount their problems with alcohol and drugs and this can often take up most of the meeting. These "drunkalogues" or stories about alcohol, make many people think of the good old days and crave alcohol even more than if they didn't go to the meeting!

Some have said that people become dependent on AA, so it's just like trading addictions. Going to meetings, the new habit, replaces the old habit of drinking, and this can be very unhealthy in and of itself. People have said that they seemed to have lost their own identity, being consumed by the AA group.

This problem will be greatest among independent minded persons.

Alcohol and drugs remain the central focus in their lives. Instead of being preoccupied with drinking, now they are completely preoccupied with NOT drinking. Now instead of remembering the good old days, they simply remember how bad things were. So they still can't break their all consuming relationship with alcohol; it's just been switched from love to hate, but they can't break away.

AA members believe they are powerless over alcohol. But according to the research, this is not true! It may be true before you quit, but you definitely show some power once you quit and even greater power the longer you stay away from it.

Members say, "Once an alcoholic, always an alcoholic." This is not exactly true. Once you've decided to quit, why wouldn't you just drop the idea that you're an alcoholic. For example, ex-smokers don't call themselves smokers once they've quit, even though the likelihood is high they'd become addicted again *if* they started smoking again. The same holds true for people with drinking or other drug problems. Some people believe, and research has shown that many people can return to normal, moderate levels of drinking if they start again and not be an alcoholic. So, in, reality, that original statement is false.

After reviewing both the positive and negative attributes of AA, and checking out a few different meetings, you can make an informed decision about what is right for you. Regardless of which treatment path you take, I want you to have as much information as possible

The National Institute of Drug Abuse, NIDA, has even gone on record to emphasize that no single addiction treatment method is right for everyone. They claim that matching treatment services to each individual's specific needs is critical to success. In addition, research studies indicate that even the most severely addicted individuals can participate actively in their own treatment, and that active participation is essential for good outcomes. According to the NIDA, counseling, either individual or group, and other behavioral therapies are critical components of effective treatment for addiction. It's interesting to note that participation in a 12-step program was never mentioned anywhere in this research based guide which discussed the principles of effective treatment.

Reliance on outdated and ineffective treatment methods has created an environment that fully expects individuals to fail, and fail again until such time that rock bottom has been reached. It is often said that once an individual has reached rock bottom there is only one way to go, UP. The problem with that philosophy is that for many people, the ultimate rock bottom is death. (Vacovsky, Executive Director, American Council on Alcoholism, May 12, 2005).

Vacovsky goes on to write:

"Many, (if not indeed most) alcohol dependent individuals have lost faith in themselves, and more importantly hope for the future. It is common for such individuals to have numerous attempts at sobriety, most often using 12-step methods. They have been *programmed* to accept themselves as hopeless and powerless, with their chance for recovery being slim to none… It is up to the individual to determine what the most appropriate treatment is. It is up to the *treatment community* to provide *options* that set up individuals to succeed, rather than be expected to fail (italics added)."

Sadly, Americans are largely unaware that such options even exist. At least, the general public is. While the public is being told that "turning your will and life over to the care of God as you understand Him," as AA suggests, is the only treatment for their illness, scientifically based research has been going on for decades. Results of this research are threefold:

1. We now have options for treatment that are based on science rather than fundamentalist religion;
2. We can give back choice and a sense of control to the individual, which is proving to be extremely important and
3. We now have evidence that is in direct contradiction to the traditional view of problem drinking.

What, exactly, is the research finding? Here is what some of the experts in the addiction field have found:

- Well-designed research conducted over more than three decades has conclusively demonstrated that problem drinking will *not* inevitably get progressively worse, and that this is one attribute of being a "disease" of alcoholism that is simply wrong. Some problem drinkers "progress," but the vast majority don't.
- What most Americans believe about drinking problems and their treatment is substantially inaccurate.
- Drinking problems do not occur as a result of a disease. It is a learned behavior, and additional learning can therefore modify behavior.
- For no other "disease" do so many physicians, psychologists and counselors themselves believe in the non-research-based myths of problem drinking, ignoring the research of their own peers in developing their treatment plans.
- "Problem drinkers in the United States are faced with a daunting dilemma when they seek help. They can either accept the prevailing myth that abstinence is the *only* effective means to resolve a drinking problem, or they can be accused of being "in denial…"
- Insistence by treatment programs to only offer abstinence has been shown to deter many problem drinkers from seeking treatment.
- Individualizing treatment is crucial.
- Chronic "relapsers" can actually be harmed by the 12-step model view that once a slip has started, you are powerless to stop. The stronger one's belief in this is, the longer and more damaging the relapses are.
- The confronting and treating of alcoholics and addicts as children, commonly thought necessary to help them, actually often hinders any change.
- Many providers deliberately resist change because they have too

much of an attachment to their own ideas of what *should* work, claiming, "I know what worked for me, and I'm sure that it can work for everyone else as long as they just do what I say."

- The only way to resolve a problem with alcohol is to abstain for life is wrong for the majority of people. A substantial proportion becomes moderate drinkers even when achieving abstinence is the primary focus of treatment.
- Dr. Patricia Owen, Director of Research of the Hazelden Foundation, who was a long-time supporter of abstinence-only treatment, referred to these individuals as "in recovery without abstinence" and acknowledged their presence in large numbers among a sample of Hazelden graduates.

Of course, not even all scientists agree on the nature of and best treatments for alcohol abuse. But this is the twenty-first century. No one would disagree that all patients suffering with an alcohol or drug problem have a right, just like any other patient suffering with any other problem, to be fully informed of the available options, the risks or areas of uncertainty, and, after reviewing the relevant information, in consultation with one or more providers, choose a course of action. This is simply good medicine. Should problem drinkers accept anything less?

It is finally time to stop living in the dark ages of recovery, educate people about all the choices and alternatives that are out there and maybe start making a dent in the alcohol and drug use problem that millions are facing each day instead of continuing to perpetuate it. If you are one of those people who still believes that the 12-steps are the "only way" to recover, I implore you to please keep an open mind. In fact, Bill W., one of the co-founders of AA said, "It would be a product of false pride to claim that A.A. is a cure-all, even for alcoholism." Bill W. repeatedly said that "our hats are off to you if you can find a better way" and "If [those seeking a different cure] can do better by other means, we are glad."

It is important to note that recovery programs are not necessary to discover how to quit and stay quit. The following is from the Harvard Medical School's *Mental Health Letter*, the August/September 1996 issue:

Most recovery from alcoholism is not the result of treatment. Only 20% of alcohol abusers are ever treated… Alcohol addicts, like heroin addicts, have a tendency to mature out of their addiction…

In a group of self-treated alcoholics, more than half said that they had simply thought it over and decided that alcohol was bad for them. Another group said health problems and frightening experiences such as accidents and blackouts persuaded them to quit… Others have recovered by changing their circumstances with the help of a new job or a new love or under the threat of a legal crisis or the breakup of a family.

Study results from addiction researchers, Doctors Linda and Mark Sobell, confirm Harvard's 20% treatment statistic:

Surveys found that over 77 percent of those who had overcome an alcohol problem had done so without treatment. In an earlier study... a sizable majority of alcohol abusers, 82 percent, recovered on their own.

However, even though it is possible to recover on your own, you may want a recovery program, or at least a licensed professional for support. That is why I have provided you with options, options that don't threaten you with "jails, institutions or death" if you don't completely follow their path. I have divided this book into seven sections. First I have described the major self-help alternatives to AA. Next, I go on to describe alternative treatment modalities. Section III is for the family members and loved ones. In Section IV, I list the top and bottom 10 treatments for alcohol abuse, taken from the most exhaustive review of alcohol treatment literature available. Then you will discover how to choose a treatment program. The last two parts are a directory. I have listed professionals who are registered with SMART, cognitive behavioral therapists, those who provide training in moderate drinking and finally, what makes this publication the first of its kind, I have listed, described and given contact information for over 100 treatment centers, both in the US and abroad, that go beyond using just the traditional 12-step approach.

SECTION I

Self-Help Groups
PART ONE: TOTAL ABSTINENCE

SAVE OUR SELVES (SOS)

SOS was the first large-scale alternative to AA. SOS was founded by James Christopher in 1985, an alcoholic himself who quit drinking in 1978, who early on in his recovery recognized that AA was not for him. SOS respects recovery in any form, regardless of the path by which it is achieved. It is not opposed to or in competition with any other recovery programs. SOS supports healthy skepticism and encourages the use of the scientific method to understand alcoholism; it does not limit its outlook to one area of knowledge or theory of addiction. All those who sincerely seek sobriety are welcome as members in any SOS Group. Although SOS believes sobriety is an individual responsibility, life does not have to be faced alone. In fact, SOS believes that the support of other alcoholics and addicts is a vital adjunct to recovery. In SOS, members share experiences, insights, information, strength and encouragement in friendly, honest, anonymous and supportive group meetings.

SOS believes that sobriety must be a priority for its members and that they must accepts that drinking or using, no matter what the circumstances, is no longer an option for them. Each member is responsible for achieving and maintaining his or her own sobriety, without reliance on any "Higher Power." In addition, members learn about the cycle of addiction and replace it with the cycle of sobriety. Here are the SOS Guidelines for Sobriety:

To break the cycle of denial and achieve sobriety, we first acknowledge that we are alcoholics or addicts. We re-affirm this truth daily and accept without reservations that, as clean and sober individuals, we can not and do not drink or use, no matter what. Since drinking or using is not an option for us, we take whatever steps are necessary to continue our Sobriety Priority lifelong. A quality of life, "the good life" can be achieved. However, life is also filled with uncertainties. Therefore, we do not drink or use regardless of feelings, circumstances, or conflicts. We share in confidence with each other our thoughts and feelings as sober, clean individuals. Sobriety is our Priority, and we are each responsible for our lives and our sobriety.

Today there are SOS groups meeting nationally, as well as in other countries. SOS has gained recognition from rehabilitation professionals and the nation's court systems. In November of 1987, the California courts recognized SOS as an alternative to AA in sentencing offenders to mandatory participation in a rehabilitation program. Also, the Veterans Administration has adopted a policy which prohibits mandatory participation in programs of a religious nature.

SOS does have a "tool kit," which is available online and which includes numerous cognitive and behavioral relapse-prevention techniques. If you would like more information about SOS, please visit www.secularsobriety.org and www.sossobriety.org. There is also a book called *The Sobriety Handbook: The*

SOS Way: An Introduction to Secular Organizations for Sobriety/Save Ourselves, which offers members techniques for staying sober. For information about a group in your area, you can call (323) 666-4295, or email them at SOS@CFIWest.org, or send them regular mail to SOS Clearinghouse (Save Our Selves) 4773 Hollywood Blvd. Hollywood, CA 90027 USA.

"SMART RECOVERY" PROGRAM

SMART Recovery® stands for Self-Management And Recovery Training. This system provides a set of tools to use and there are free meetings both online and face-to-face to learn, practice and refine these skills. SMART emphasized four points:

1. Motivation to Abstain – Enhancing and maintaining motivation to abstain from addictive behavior;
2. Coping with Urges – Learning how to cope with urges and cravings;
3. Problem Solving-Using rational ways to manage thoughts, feelings and behaviors and
4. Lifestyle Balance – Balancing short-term and long-term pleasures and satisfactions in life.

SMART is based on Rational Emotive Behavior Therapy (REBT), which was developed by Dr. Albert Ellis in the 1950's. Ellis stated there are three aspects of human functioning: thoughts, feelings and behavior. His proposal was that thinking creates feelings and actions. In other words, people or events don't make us feel good or bad; it is our *perception* of them that result in our feeling good or bad. And these perceptions then influence our behavior.

SMART views addiction as a bad habit. It does _not_ view it as a disease, and therefore, there are no labels used, such as "alcoholics" or "addicts." SMART is supported by research on relapse prevention, motivational enhancement and behavioral change processes. It emphasizes self-responsibility, self-motivation and self-discipline as the primary means of stopping substance use. Unlike AA, SMART meetings do not dwell on past "war stories." They focus on present day events and the causes of self-destructive behaviors. There are no "sponsors" in SMART, and anyone can attend these meetings who wants to deal with a compulsive behavior, whether it's gambling, pills, shopping, or others.

One of the major tools used in SMART is called the "ABC process," which is a method to identify and dispute our irrational beliefs, thoughts and feelings. By doing this, new rational beliefs, thoughts and feelings can replace the old. In addition, they believe this helps to resist urges and regain control.

SMART also uses a cost-benefit analysis as another tool. They propose that it helps to build motivation to abstain from using by creating goals, developing coping skills, and pointing out relapse warning signs.

If you want to learn more about this tool and this Program in general, including online or face-to-face meetings, literature, or talking to a live person, please go to www.smartrecovery.org or call them at (216) 292-0220. You can also write them at 24000 Mercantile Rd., Suite 11, Beachwood, Ohio 44122. You can also visit the Ellis Institute at www.albertellisinstitute.org/aei/index.html. You can find a therapist registered with SMART in Section Two. For the most current meeting list nationwide, go to www.smartrecovery.org/meetings/outline.htm.

LIFERING SECULAR RECOVERY

LifeRing believes that there are as many different ways to get clean and sober as there are alcoholics and addicts. In other words, **there is no magic formula that works for everyone at all times**. All of the different "Programs" out there contain some useful ideas. Every method produces some success stories. Every method produces some relapses. Therefore, the LifeRing approach to recovery emphasizes learning through experimentation.

According to the LifeRing approach, you will try different ideas and different behaviors and see if they help keep you sober. If they work for you, you will probably keep them; if they lead you into relapse, you are encouraged to change them and try something else. And if you fall, LifeRing will *** not try to shame you*** or make you feel that you were not following "The Program" (there is none). In fact, they feel just the opposite: a relapse may be a key part of your learning experience. (You find out one more thing that does not work for you). The set of ideas and behaviors you find that work for you make up your own personal recovery program. Makes common sense, doesn't it?

The basic LifeRing philosophy can be summed up in three words: Sobriety, Secularity, and Self-Help.

- **Sobriety** means abstinence from alcohol and other medically non-indicated addictive drugs. In LifeRing, people struggling with a variety of drugs – alcohol, marijuana, methamphetamines, cocaine, heroin, prescription drugs, to name a few – work side by side. LifeRing respects the doctor-patient relationship. If you have been honest with your doctor, you will get support in taking your medications as prescribed.
- **Secularity** means that your religion or lack of it remains your private business. Whether you believe in a Supreme Being is not important in LifeRing. Meetings do not use prayer or discuss theology, pro or con. What *is* important is that each person takes responsibility for his or her own recovery and is available to give support to others.
- **Self-Help** means that each person develops a personal recovery program tailored to his or her particular background and needs. Other than "Don't drink or Use," LifeRing does not believe in a prescribed set of steps that everyone needs to follow. Because there is not "One Program," you do not need a special sponsor to guide you. Instead, they all help each other. Self-help also means that meetings are led by peers, not by professionals.

LifeRing offers a wide variety of online support options, including chat rooms, email lists, e-pals and a bulletin board. If you would like more information on LifeRing, or to access any of these options, please visit www.unhooked.com. You can contact LifeRing by email, service@lifering.org, or you can call them at (510)763-0779 or toll free at (800) 811-4142. The most current meeting list can be found at www.unhooked.com/meetings/index.html.

RATIONAL RECOVERY

Another alternative to AA is Rational Recovery (RR), which was founded in 1986 by Jack Trimpey. Trimpey was also an alcoholic who disliked AA, so much to the point of attacking AA, and being devoted to political action aimed at ending the recovery movement. As a result, RR may be particularly helpful to those who find AA and treatment downright offensive, rather than not right for them.

This Method does not require belief in a higher power. It does not involve any counseling, therapy, meetings, psychology, or spirituality. RR views these as personal matters that have nothing to do with sobriety. RR believes that the worst way to quit something you love is one day at a time.

RR believes that all that is needed to acquire and maintain sobriety is a method of "planned abstinence" using their approach called addictive voice recognition technique (AVRT), based on the experiences of former addicts. According to RR, AVRT is a simple thinking skill that helps addicts recognize and resist the internal "voice", (the *Beast*) that pressures them to use chemicals for their effect, which is the sole cause of addiction, once and for all. The addictive voice is called The Beast because it is believed to be the voice of the lower, or what RR calls the "animal" parts of the brain. What RR sees as the voice of the Beast runs along the same lines as what AA calls the voice of the disease and what cognitive-behavioral therapists call craving.

The RR program was originally based on a type of cognitive therapy called rational emotive behavior therapy (REBT), created by Albert Ellis, but has now been rejected, along with all kinds of "psychological" approaches, such as treatment, counseling or therapy. AVRT alone is believed to be enough to end addiction without any other psychological changes. According to Trimpey, reading about AVRT in the RR book, *Rational Recovery*, and attending two to three meetings should be sufficient to learn what you need to know. rR proponents believe that "meetings", identifying with other alcoholics or addicts, is actually part of the problem and therefore not helpful to recovery.

For more information, please go to the website at www.rational.org. On their website, you will find discussion groups, chat lines, email services and newsgroups. Trimpey also offers a four-day AVRT course in Northern California. For more information, call (530) 621-4374.

PENNSYLVANIA MODEL-MEDICATION PLUS COGNITIVE BEHAVIORAL THERAPY

According to the American Council on Alcoholism, the Center for Substance Abuse Treatment, the Substance Abuse and Mental Health Services Administration, (SAMHSA), and many other research findings, show that medications, such as Naltrexone or Acamprosate, help people who have been abusing alcohol to at least moderate their drinking. "Since craving is a neuro-chemical reaction, it is best treated with medications." (Menzies, Director, Assisted Recovery Centers of Missouri, American Council on Alcoholism, May 12, 2005). The FDA first approved Naltrexone in 1984 under the brand name Trexan for the treatment of opiate abuse. In 1994, the FDA extended its use to include alcohol dependence. Dr. Joseph Volpicelli, of the University Of Pennsylvania School Of Medicine, has been conducting research on Naltrexone use for alcohol dependence since the early 1980s.

Dr. Volpicelli explains that the benefits of this drug are not so much in preventing taking that first drink, but rather in breaking the cycle of excessive drinking.

According to Lloyd Vacovsky, the executive director of the American Council on Alcoholism, the use of Naltrexone, and/or Acamprosate, a newer drug which is approved for the treatment of alcoholism in many European countries and has now been approved by the FDA, can be very effective tools, when appropriately used, because they can suppress the intense craving to drink or use. However, medications are not to be used as an unaccompanied treatment, but as a useful addition to a more comprehensive plan.

This brings us to the **Pennsylvania Model of Recovery,** which is the use of medication, such as Naltrexone, *in addition to* Cognitive Behavioral Therapy to address the Psychological and Social parts of recovery. This model is based largely on the research and work of the University Of Pennsylvania School Of Medicine, Treatment Research Center, in Philadelphia, and in particular, Dr. Joseph R. Volpicelli, M.D., Ph.D., also of the University Of Pennsylvania. This Model does not require any acceptance of a "Higher Power" in order for you to recover.

The Pennsylvania Model views alcohol dependence as an acute disorder of the pleasure center of the brain. It is treated as a bio-psycho-social condition, rather than as a lack of character, or as a "spiritual disease." The physical component is treated with the medicine, Naltrexone, which eliminates the physical cravings normally associated with abstinence from alcohol. According to this Model, with the cravings under control, you can now deal with the psychological and social components of the addiction. In other words, you need to learn to change the way you think about certain things and the social habits that you spent your whole life developing. This is where Cognitive Behavioral Therapy (CBT), Motivational Enhancement Therapy (MET) and Rational Emotive Behavior Therapy (REBT) come into play. The Pennsylvania Model believes that using the tools of the above therapies, you will learn to:

- Set and achieve reasonable goals
- Enhance motivation to stay abstinent
- Deal with life's problems effectively
- Prevent lapse from becoming a relapse
- Develop a more healthy lifestyle
- Learn to enjoy life without alcohol or drugs

With this model, treatment is started with four basic assumptions:
- Addiction is a chronic disease characterized by a tendency to relapse.
- Those who begin treatment and stay in treatment generally get better.
- A variety of biological, psychological and social factors lead to addiction, and these factors also offer strategies for recovery.
- Individualized treatment programs are more effective than those that offer a "one-size-fits-all" approach.

Along with REBT, CBT and MET, they combine medications, self-help and good medical practice. Their system has 6 components, which can be remembered through the acronym BRENDA:

B- Biopsychosocial Evaluation (Assessment)

R- Report to patient on assessment

E- Empathetic understanding of the patient's situation, offering necessary support

N- Needs (a determination of key needs to be met in ore=der to achieve recovery)

D- Direct advice to the patient on how to meet those needs

A- Assessment of reaction of patient to advice and changes in strategy to address problems.

This treatment program will fit the treatment to the individual and not the other way around. They attempt to take their approach to the individual's particular and unique needs. This model, using the research findings on relapse prevention, find it very important to distinguish between a small slip, (i.e. you have a glass of wine), and a huge relapse involving excessive use. This is due to the fact that people have so much shame about relapsing, they often let a small slip become much more serious because they've figured they've blown it all anyway. By using this notion of slips, they allow people to feel that recovery doesn't end with just one mistake, but there are a series of decisions involved, which can be stopped at any point. The bottom line is that they try to remove the shame attached to relapsing, and treat slips and relapses as learning opportunities.

Assisted Recovery Centers of America (ARCA) was the first in the nation to offer a non 12-step program of recovery from alcohol dependence using the Pennsylvania Model of Recovery. While there is no spiritual component in this Model, ARCA does encourage clients who are inclined to add a "spiritual" component to their recovery to attend AA, or the church of their choice. ARCA now offer an opiate addiction treatment with Suboxone, using this same Model.

ARCA has four programs to choose from, including one online. This includes a weekly online chat session and private email group, plus telephone access to their counselors and staff. If you would like more information on this Model of Recovery, or ARCA, please visit them at www.assistedrecovery.com. You can also call them at (602) 264-7897 or toll free at (800) 527-5344, for their Phoenix, Arizona location. You can call (314) 645-6840, for their St. Louis, Missouri location, or email them at contactus@arcamidwest.com.

PART TWO: PROGRAMS DESIGNED BY WOMEN, FOR WOMEN (Adapted now for men, too)

WOMEN FOR SOBRIETY (Also has MEN FOR SOBRIETY)

Another alternative is called, "Women for Sobriety," or "WFS." Unfunded by any agency, WFS is a non-profit organization that was started in 1975 by Jean Kirkpatrick, an alcoholic who felt like AA was not right for her due to the male bias of AA. According to WFS, they are dedicated to helping women overcome alcoholism and other addictions through the discovery of self, gained by sharing experiences, hopes and encouragement with other women in similar circumstances. WFS believes that drinking began to overcome stress, loneliness, frustration, emotional deprivation, or any number of other kinds of harassment from which dependence and addiction resulted. WFS believes that this physiological addiction can only be overcome by abstinence, and that mental and emotional addiction are overcome with the knowledge of self gained through this program. Members of WFS live by the WFS philosophy: forget the past, plan for tomorrow, and live today.

As a Program, it can stand alone or be used along with other programs simultaneously. It is being used not only by women alcoholics in small self-help groups but also in hospitals, clinics, treatment facilities, women centers, and wherever alcoholics are being treated. (Since the inception of WFS in 1976, many men began requesting the Program and Men For Sobriety groups have formed around the United States and throughout Canada).

You might be asking why a recovery program was started just for women. Until the founding of WFS, it was assumed that any program for recovery from alcoholism would work equally well for women as for men. When it became obvious that recovery rates for male alcoholics were higher than for females, it was then declared that women were harder to treat and less cooperative than males. WFS came forth with the belief that women alcoholics require a different kind of program in recovery than the traditional kinds of programs used for male alcoholics (The Big Book of Alcoholics Anonymous was written in the 1930's by men, mainly for men.). The psychological and emotional needs for women are very different in recovery from those of the male alcoholic.

So, what exactly is this "New Life" Program? It is based upon a Thirteen Statement Program of positivity and acceptance, which I have listed below so you can get an idea of this Program and determine if it resonates with you.

"NEW LIFE" ACCEPTANCE PROGRAM

1. **I have a life-threatening problem that once had me.** *I now take charge of my life. I accept the responsibility.*
2. **Negative thoughts destroy only myself.** *My first conscious act must be to remove negativity from my life.*
3. **Happiness is a habit I will develop.** *Happiness is created, not waited*

for.

4. **Problems bother me only to the degree I permit them to.** *I now better understand my problems and do not permit problems to overwhelm me.*
5. **I am what I think.** *I am a capable, competent, caring, compassionate woman.*
6. **Life can be ordinary or it can be great.** *Greatness is mine by a conscious effort.*
7. **Love can change the course of my world.** *Caring becomes all important.*
8. **The fundamental object of life is emotional and spiritual growth.** *Daily I put my life into a proper order, knowing which are the priorities.*
9. **The past is gone forever.** *No longer will I be victimized by the past; I am a new person.*
10. **All love given returns.** *I will learn to know that others love me.*
11. **Enthusiasm is my daily exercise.** *I treasure all moments of my new life.*
12. **I am a competent woman and have much to give life.** *This is what I am and I shall know it always.*
13. **I am responsible for myself and for my actions.** *I am in charge of my mind, my thoughts, and my life.*

For more information about this Program, please visit www.womenforsobriety.org. You can also email them at NewLife@nni.com or call (215) 536-8026 to talk with someone in person who can answer any questions you may have, including the locations of meetings.

16-STEP FOR DISCOVERY AND EMPOWERMENT MODEL

The 16-step empowerment model is a holistic approach to overcoming addiction that views people in their entirety – mind, body and spirit. Created by Charlotte Kasl, Ph.D., this model was based on hundreds of her interviews with counselors and those in recovery treatment programs across the country. From her findings, she believes that people develop addictions for many reasons, and heal in different ways. Dr. Kasl states:

> In the traditional 12-step approach to addiction (known as Alcoholics Anonymous), basic assumptions about addiction and addicted people are based on observations, made over 50 years ago, of *100 white, primarily upper middle class, professional men who were alcoholics.* These theories were then adopted, without examination, for a multitude of other addictions and problems, and presented routinely to people of different races and social strata as the *one and only way to overcome addiction.* The 16-step model helps people to develop ego strength which is seen as having a healthy ability to be introspective and to ask oneself the questions: Who am I? What do I value, believe and want?" (Kasl, *16-Steps for Discovery and Empowerment*)

In this model, addiction is seen as complex, encompassing social factors, physical factors, pre-disposition and personal history. This method believes that a major task in recovering from addiction is to validate the underlying, positive survival goals for safety, connection, pleasure, love and power that using used to accomplish, and then to find non-addictive and positive ways to meet those needs. This model also addresses issues of cultural diversity and internalized oppression stemming from sexism, racism, classism and homophobia because the steps are all about empowerment.

The 16 steps that follow are published in *Many Roads, One Journey: Moving Beyond the 12 Steps* and in *Yes, You Can! A Guide to Empowerment Groups.* "As you read these steps, remember that models and concepts are just that – models and concepts. They are words and ideas... Just as the menu is not the meal, the 12-steps are not recovery, neither are the thirteen steps of Women for Sobriety, or the 16 empowerment steps I have put together. They are ideas about recovery. They are words written by people reflecting their observations and experiences. So take these 16 steps, experiment with them, change them, skip them, or write your own. Live in the heart in your own life." (Dr. Kasl, *Zen, Feminism, and Recovery: 16 Steps for Discovery and Empowerment*, 2/5/05). These steps are currently in use in an estimated 200-300 groups nationwide, as well as a rapidly growing number of treatment programs.

The 16-Steps:

1. We affirm we have the power to take charge of our lives and stop being

dependent on substances or other people for our self-esteem and security.
 – *Alternative:* We admit/acknowledge we are out of control with/powerless over _____ yet have the power to take charge of our lives and stop being dependent on substances or other people for our self-esteem and security.
2. **(New version of this step)** We come to believe that we have the ability to develop our inner resources through a process of learning, exploration, daily practice, diligence, self reflection, and supportive relationships with others.
 – **(Old version of this step)** We come to believe that God/Goddess/Universe/Great Spirit/Higher Power awakens the healing wisdom within us when we open ourselves to the power.
3. We make a decision to become our authentic selves and trust in the healing power of the truth.
4. We examine our beliefs, addictions and dependent behavior in the context of living in a hierarchical, patriarchal culture.
5. We share with another person and the Universe all those things inside of us for which we feel shame and guilt.
6. We affirm and enjoy our intelligence, strengths and creativity, remembering not to hide these qualities from ourselves and others.
7. We become willing to let go of shame, guilt, and any behavior that keeps us from loving ourselves and others.
8. We make a list of people we have harmed and people who have harmed us, and take steps to clear out negative energy by making amends and sharing our grievances in a respectful way.
9. We express love and gratitude to others and increasingly appreciate the wonder of life and the blessings we do have.
10. We learn to trust our reality and daily affirm that we see what we see, we know what we know and we feel what we feel.
11. We promptly admit to mistakes and make amends when appropriate, but we do not say we are sorry for things we have not done and we do not cover up, analyze, or take responsibility for the shortcomings of others.
12. We seek out situations, jobs, and people who affirm our intelligence, perceptions and self-worth and avoid situations or people who are hurtful, harmful, or demeaning to us.
13. We take steps to heal our physical bodies, organize our lives, reduce stress, and have fun.
14. We seek to find our inward calling, and develop the will and wisdom to follow it.
15. We accept the ups and downs of life as natural events that can be used as lessons for our growth.
16. We grow in awareness that we are sacred beings, interrelated with all living things, and we contribute to restoring peace and balance on the planet.

If you would like more information about the 16-step model, please visit www.charlottekasl.com. You can also write to Dr. Kasl at Many Roads One Journey, Inc. PO Box 1302 Lolo, Montana 59847. You can find the most current national meeting list by going to www.charlottekasl.com/programs.html.

PART THREE: MODERATION

MODERATION MANAGEMENT

According to the National Institute on Alcohol Abuse and Alcoholism, and many other independent researchers, there are four times as many problem drinkers as alcoholics in this country. Yet there are very few programs that specifically address the needs of beginning stage problem drinkers. By the time people reach serious stages of alcohol dependency, changing drinking habits becomes more difficult. MM believes that this situation needs to be remedied in the interest of public health and human kindness with early intervention and harm reduction programs.

According to MM, nine out of ten problem drinkers today actively and purposefully avoid traditional treatment approaches. MM believes this is because they know that most traditional programs will label them as "alcoholic," probably force attendance at 12-step meetings, and prescribe lifetime abstinence as the only acceptable change in drinking. Traditional approaches that are based on the disease model of alcohol dependence and its reliance on the concept of powerlessness can be particularly counterproductive for women and minorities, who often already feel like victims and powerless. Outcome studies indicate that professional programs, which offer both moderation and abstinence have *higher* success rates than those that offer abstinence only. Clients tend to self-select the behavior change options which will work best for them.

MM is a behavioral change program and national support group network for people concerned about their drinking and who desire to make positive lifestyle changes. MM agrees with many professionals and researchers in the field that alcohol abuse, versus dependence, is a learned behavior (habit) for problem drinkers, and *not* a disease. MM empowers individuals to accept personal responsibility for choosing and maintaining their own path, whether moderation or abstinence. MM promotes early self-recognition of risky drinking behavior, when moderate drinking is a more easily achievable goal. Seriously dependent drinkers will probably find a return to moderate drinking a great challenge, but the choice to accept that challenge remains theirs.

MM is a 9-step professionally reviewed program, which provides information about alcohol, moderate drinking guidelines and limits, drink monitoring exercises, goal setting techniques and self-management strategies. Here are the nine steps toward moderation and positive lifestyle changes:

1. Attend meetings or on-line groups and learn about the program of Moderation Management.
2. Abstain from alcoholic beverages for 30 days and complete steps three through six during this time.
3. Examine how drinking has affected your life.
4. Write down your life priorities.
5. Take a look at how much, how often, and under what circumstances you had been drinking.

6. Learn the MM guidelines and limits for moderate drinking.
7. Set moderate drinking limits and start weekly "small steps" toward balance and moderation in other areas of your life.
8. Review your progress and update your goals.
9. Continue to make positive lifestyle changes and attend meetings whenever you need ongoing support or would like to help newcomers.

MM's suggested guidelines below allow for a degree of individual interpretation because moderation is a flexible principle and is not the same for everyone. MM's suggested limits, however, are more definite.

A Moderate Drinker:
- Considers an occasional drink to be a small, though enjoyable, part of life.
- Has hobbies, interests, and other ways to relax and enjoy life that do not involve alcohol.
- *Usually* has friends who are moderate drinkers or nondrinkers.
- *Generally* has something to eat before, during, or soon after drinking.
- *Usually* does not drink for longer than an hour or two on any particular occasion.
- *Usually* does not drink faster than one drink per half-hour.
- *Usually* does not exceed the .055% BAC moderate drinking limit.
- Feels comfortable with his or her use of alcohol (never drinks secretly and does not spend a lot of time thinking about drinking or planning to drink).

The MM Limits:
- Strictly obey local laws regarding drinking and driving.
- Do not drink in situations that would endanger yourself or others.
- Do not drink every day. MM suggests that you abstain from drinking alcohol at least 3 or 4 days per week.
- Women, who drink more than 3 drinks on any day, and more than 9 drinks per week, may be drinking at harmful levels.
- Men, who drink more than 4 drinks on any day, and more than 14 drinks per week, may be drinking at harmful levels.

The limits used by MM are based on research published in 1995 in the *American Journal of Public Health*, by Dr. Martha Sanchez-Craig, Addiction Research Foundation, Toronto, Canada and other published limits.

After completing the 30 days of abstinence and then starting the moderation part of the program, you may discover that it is more difficult for you to moderate your drinking than to abstain. In this case, MM says to consider a self-management goal of abstinence. Some members of MM who choose abstinence remain in MM; others find an abstinence-only group to attend, such as any of the one's I have mentioned in the first part of this booklet.

MM is *not* for every person with a drinking problem. If MM proves to be an ineffective solution, you are encouraged to progress to a more radical solution. To decide if this program is for you, MM suggests that you take into account the severity of your drinking problem, your personal preference, and any medical, psychological, or other conditions that would be made worse by drinking, even in moderation. MM does not provide professional assessment or treatment.

If you want to learn more about this program, please visit www.moderation.org, call MM at (212) 871-0974 or email them at mm@moderation.org. To find out if you are considered to have a low, medium or high dependence on alcohol, take MM's short alcohol dependence data questionnaire at www.moderation.org/Questionnaire.shtml. See Section Two for therapists who provide training in moderate drinking. The list is current as of March 14, 2005. You can find a MM meeting in your area by going to www.moderation.org/natlf2f.shtml. This meeting directory is current as of May 23, 2005.

THE SINCLAIR METHOD: MEDICATION PLUS EXTINCTION OF LEARNED BEHAVIOR

The Sinclair Method is based on some of the scientific findings made over the past 25 years by Dr. David Sinclair in his research at the National Public Health Institute in Finland. Dr. Sinclair was born in the United States, but has lived and worked in Finland for the past 30 years. He was one of the first researchers to question the disease concept of alcoholism, and to document through experiments and animal studies that the act of drinking is, in fact, a learned behavior, and *not* a disease, that becomes progressively stronger with repetition and experience.

According to the Sinclair Method, drinking tends to be learned slowly, over a period of years. The brain produces natural opiates when alcohol is consumed and it is the act of releasing these natural opiates that produces the "high" or feelings of enjoyment. The brain begins to crave more and more alcohol. In other words, too much drinking leads to the production of too many natural opiates, so that over a period of time, it takes more alcohol to produce those same feelings of enjoyment that you had in the beginning. The brain begins to crave more and more alcohol. Sinclair believes that this process of drinking and craving can be reversed partly or wholly through the process of extinction.

Dr. Sinclair was also one of the first to recognize how the use of Naltrexone can lead to an extinction, or elimination, of the craving for alcohol. Neurons in the brain release endorphins when alcohol is present. Certain prescription medications are now proven to block the reinforcement from endorphins. In other words, extinction occurs when alcohol is consumed while the reinforcement (the "high") is blocked. So, according to Sinclair, by following this method, drinking and craving are extinguished, and this method can be used whether your goal is to moderate your drinking, or to stop drinking completely.

If you want to learn more about the Sinclair Method, please visit www.sinclairmethod.com. Or if you are interested in a treatment center that offers the Sinclair Method or the Pennsylvania Model, depending on which one you feel is best for you, please visit www.newerahealthcenter.com. Or you can email them at clinical@newerahealthcenter.com or call them at (305) 559-8838. You can also get in touch with Neurobehavioral Medicine Centers, which also uses the Sinclair Method. Their website is www.sinclairmethod.com, call them at (941) 321-4104 or email them at beverlyrayfield@earthlink.net. Both centers are located in Florida.

PART FOUR: HARM REDUCTION THERAPY

Harm reduction therapy, HRT, is a motivational approach to increase people's desire for greater health and well-being. It does *not* believe that addiction is a disease, but rather a biopsychosocial phenomenon. In other words, one must look at biological, physiological, psychological, emotional and social factors in such a way that each person's relationship with drugs and alcohol is completely unique. Presented by Patt Denning, Ph.D. and Jeannie Little, LCSW, both psychotherapists and addiction specialists, HRT is a combination of proven effective treatment methods developed by other specialists in the fields of mental health and substance abuse. Treatment is tailored to the individual, *not* the individual to the treatment.

This approach starts where the person is in their struggle with drugs and alcohol, and works from the principles of acceptance and empowerment. Instead of the goal being abstinence, it is improved quality of life, in such areas as mental health, homelessness, incarceration, employment and disease transmission. Research has shown that many people reduce the harm by learning more about drugs and alcohol and by developing strategies to manage their usage.

Denning et al writes:

"Harm reduction means taking control-of your use of drugs or alcohol, of the damage that use does to you, of the harm your use causes others and of how you live your life. It means looking closely at the role alcohol or drugs play in your survival, your ability to function, your capacity to cope with the pain you suffer and your enjoyment of life's pleasure. It is a means by which you can change the way you use alcohol or other drugs, either by quitting or moderating, to reduce the harm your use causes, whether that involves, for example, drinking less or less often or using milder drugs. It is a means to make your own decisions about how much change you need or can tolerate. Harm reduction does not encourage you to hand over the decision making to others. If your decisions lead you to quit, either now or later, fine. If you don't quit, that's fine too. As long as you make *any* change that reduces harm, you're practicing harm reduction, and you're moving in a positive direction. *Any Positive Change* is the motto of harm reduction."

HRT claims to be particularly well-suited to those who have tried abstinence-based approaches and found them to be ineffective or undesirable, relapse frequently, and have other emotional or psychological problems that do not get sufficient or well-integrated treatment, and/or prefer an alternative way of thinking about addiction.

If you would like more information on harm reduction therapy, please visit the harm reduction coalition's website at www.harmreductiontherapy.org. HRC is committed to reducing drug-related harm among individuals and communities by initiating and promoting local, regional and national harm reduction education, interventions and community organizing. HRC fosters alternative models to conventional drug treatments and believes in every individuals right to health and well-being as well as in their competency to protect and help themselves and their loved ones. Feel free to email them at info@harmreductiontherapy.org or call 415-863-4282. (See Harm Reduction Therapy Center in Third Section for Outpatient Services.)

SECTION II
Alternative Treatments

Note: These may or may not work all on their own, or they may need to be joined as a supplement to something else. You just need to get your own personal experience with these and find what resonates with you because each person is unique.

ACUPUNCTURE

Acupuncture is an Eastern medicine technique that has been utilized for centuries. American interest in the technique was sparked in the 1970s when a Hong Kong neurosurgeon operating on an opium addict was getting ready to use electro-acupuncture as a method of surgical analgesia. The patient happened to also report a relief in symptoms of withdrawal. This was then tested on many future patients who also testified in experiencing less symptoms of withdrawal. Acupuncture, the insertion of hair-thin needless under the skin, may also relieve cravings for alcohol as well as alleviate some of the symptoms of alcohol withdrawal, such as tremors and fatigue. It may also reduce anxiety and depression, which lead some people to drink alcohol or use drugs.

One of the reasons that acupuncture helps to relieve symptoms is because endorphins, our natural pain-killing body chemical, are released. Endorphins tend to reduce cravings, ease symptoms of withdrawal and also tend to increase feelings of relaxation. When a person has a long history of addiction, the endorphin generating system in their brain has been damaged by the overuse of the external drug that is similar to the endorphin in chemical structure. In these cases, internal endorphin generation is decreased. Acupuncture stimulates endorphin generation and can calm the central nervous system, relieve the stress, help with anxiety and depression and give the patient a greater sense of well-being. This aids in relieving the mind of the psychological craving for drugs and alcohol. Chen continuing a course of acupuncture treatment, the addicted person's very weak generation of endorphins is gradually restored to a normal level. After recovery, the endorphin generation system should remain strong enough to prevent relapse. In other words, the patient no longer has the physical craving for the drug.

Michael Smith, of Lincoln Hospital Center in The Bronx, pioneered acupuncture treatment for addiction in America. His center currently treats 250 addicts every day with auricular acupuncture and counseling. Smith claims that between 50 and 75 percent of his patients continue treatment for three months and are clean at the end of the program, a rate that is comparable to other treatments.

Acupuncture encourages the body to promote natural healing and improve functioning. This is done with the insertion of the fine needles and the application of heat or electrical stimulation to precise acupuncture points of the body. In ancient China, doctors discovered that there are 14 major acupuncture channels in the body, involving over 700 different points distributed all over the surface of the skin, which individually connect different organs and other tissues. The qi (pronounced chee) meaning vital energy, is flowing and circulating in these channels. The needles used in acupuncture work by unblocking the different channels and allowing Qi to flow freely.

In Chinese medical theory, disturbances and dysfunctions in yin (negative, yielding, dark, cold and feminine), yang (positive, dominant, bright, warm and masculine), qi and blood create all disease. Through various manipulative stimulation methods acupuncture works to adjust, balance and correct the disturbances and dysfunctions to cure illness.

Regardless of the setting, and the substance abused, acupuncture treatment aids in patient detoxification. It does so by supporting the main organs of elimination in the body, speeding the body's ability to rid itself of toxins. Treatment can improve mental clarity and ability to focus. It also has been shown to provide some people with a sense of calmness and serenity.

CHINESE HERBS

There is a growing body of research literature addressing Chinese herbal medicine from around the world, most concerning the effects of individual herbs. The fact that Chinese herbs are traditionally used in combinations tend to complicate research as we know it because more than one substance is involved and has to be considered. Considerable excitement was generated by studies at Harvard University. Scientists reported that the extracts of the herb Ge Gen (Kudzu, Pueraria) reduced alcohol consumption. A Harvard study (Keung et al, 1993) demonstrated that the active ingredient from the kudzu root, diadzin, reduced hamster alcohol consumption by 50 percent and reduced cravings. These findings were confirmed in subsequent animal and human trials.

In one study, 14 human volunteers were placed in an apartment and allowed to drink as many beers as they wanted, up to a maximum of six. This resulted in a baseline observation of how many bottles of beer each person could drink under "normal" circumstances. Then, half were given a capsule containing kudzu and half were given a placebo before another period of beer consumption. The results of this experiment were startling. Each person who took the kudzu drank significantly less alcohol than those who took the placebo. Furthermore, those in the kudzu group were both slower and less likely to request a second or third bottle of beer. The individuals in the placebo group drank three or four bottles which was on average twice as much as the individuals who took kudzu. In addition, those in the kudzu group needed more gulps and swallows to finish a bottle of beer. This led to a suggestion that kudzu may be acting on the brain and telling the body not to drink excessive amounts of alcohol.

The Pacific Complementary Medicine Center in Stockton, CA has been offering Ju Hua (Chrysanthemum) tea along with National Acupuncture Detoxification Association (NADA) ear acupuncture since 1995. Teresa M. Chen, PhD., reports that the tea was questioned because clients of the juvenile court diversion program were giving clean urine samples 99 percent of the time. Such incredibly high rates of drug-free samples made people suspect that the tea might be changing the samples. After consulting with some experts, it was concurred that the tea would not be changing the samples or masking evidence of illicit drug use. The program believes strongly in the benefits of the tea and continues to serve it.

Chinese herbs relieve the body of any remaining toxins and clean the body through various approaches, including promoting urination to drive out toxins, unblocking the bowels to drive out toxins and promoting blood and qi circulation to remove toxins from the organs and other tissues. Recent research shows that in addicted patients, Chinese herbal medicine effectively promotes and regulates microcirculation and helps to drive out toxins.

According to Dr. Ji Zhang, the staff doctor at Passages and who has written what some critics say is the most comprehensive encyclopedia of herbs ever published, Chinese herbal medicine can also calm the spirit, reduce the sensitivity of the nervous system, improve your mental condition and prevent a drug and alcohol relapse. It also restores the internal generation of endorphins, helping to relax mental tension, reduce anxiety and relieve depression. He says that the following herbs are particularly effective for detoxification:

- Pine tree leaves can invigorate blood circulation to detoxify and unblock the channels and collaterals to relieve the pain experienced during detoxification
- Licorice can detoxify, moderate anxiety and depression and relieve pain
- Dandelion can promote urination to detoxify
- Other herbs, such as Membranous Milk Vetch, Honeysuckle, Aweto Angelica and American Ginseng are also used for treating alcoholism and addiction

HYPNOTHERAPY

Hypnotherapy (the practice of Hypnosis as a therapy) is a natural state of heightened awareness, frequently associated with relaxation, where the therapist enables you, if you wish, to be more receptive to positive suggestion to help effect positive changes in your life. Hypnotherapy is guided relaxation and or concentration where the ideas (suggestions) by the therapist are generally remembered more readily, which in turn creates new awareness. Depending on the client's motivations, there may be a shift in attitude about specific subject matters (habits and stresses). A well-trained and experienced therapist can use the experiences perceived under hypnosis to desensitize a client's fears, improve his or her self-image, or gain other behavioral or emotional goals. Goal achievement is an area of human behavior where the tool of hypnosis is very helpful.

Hypnosis is a normal state of concentrated and focused attention. You experience hypnosis spontaneously several times per day, like when losing sense of time reading a book, absorbed in a TV program, or driving for hours concentrated on your thoughts. You allow your conscious mind to drift away and go to rest. Then your subconscious carries out for you an extremely larger number of activities than your conscious mind.

Different aspects of Self are in charge of specific activities. Simply put, the Subconscious is in charge of the automatic, involuntary bodily functions and actions. It stores memories, is responsible for emotions, spontaneous ideas, intuition, attitudes, self image and habits. It is "unlimited" and does not make the difference between reality and imagination. Meanwhile, the Conscious Mind solves problems with efficiency in real time and space as long as it works in the limited realm of the individual's present belief system. It is analytical, critical and logical, preventing us from making mistakes.

The conscious mind is unable to help with "rationals" in case of acute stressful events, or some lifelong suffering habits. It does not have the unlimited powers of the subconscious. Hypnotherapy is a consent situation. You work together with the therapist, to bring about changes and improve life. The therapist guides the body and conscious mind to go to rest which lets the subconscious mind come to the front, receptive to the suggestions agreed upon. With regressions, you find the roots of a problem, uncover buried memories and the causes of unwanted habits.

NUTRITION

The idea of using diet to help people recover from their addictions is a good one. It has long been known that many severe alcoholics suffer from malnutrition. Drinking depletes the body of many nutrients and alcohol itself can cause hypoglycemia (low blood sugar) 3-36 hours after drinking, which may be interpreted as a craving for alcohol rather than hunger. In addition, because people who are drinking and using tend to be more concerned with getting their substances than with eating, good dietary habits are rare, with some suffering starvation and major nutrient deficits.

The basic diet, such as what you would find with Seven Weeks to Sobriety, is rather simple. Eliminate caffeine, nicotine, sugar and white flour. Supplement your diet with antioxidants (Vitamin C & E), amino acids (particularly 5HTP) and DL phenylalanine, which are precursors to the neurotransmitters serotonin and dopamine, respectively, calcium, magnesium, pancreatic enzymes, essential fatty acids and L-glutamine.

As for the particular elements of the diet, at least one has been subjected to some research with some positive conclusive evidence. That is on L-glutamine, an amino acid available at health food stores, which may help reduce cravings for alcohol. Studies done as far back as the 1950s reported positive effects; one rat study found that it decreased the animal's alcohol intake by 34 percent. There have also been case reports on the increased ability to sleep normally, and even, for some, a return to control over alcohol drinking. Promoters of nutritional programs report similar effects from L-glutamine today, but there still hasn't been a good study that would clarify whether these effects are better than placebo. Please be informed: If you wish to take L-glutamine and you have liver disease, consult your doctor first because those with very serious types of this disease can be harmed by it.

It is up to you if you want to experiment with diets to aid your recovery. There is no evidence that any of the above suggestions are harmful, but like many other treatments, they are unlikely to be a miracle cure and may offer no help at all. Also, some people may find it frustrating or intolerable to try such a restricted diet soon after quitting alcohol or drugs. When you have just given up your main source of comfort, it's a good idea to be easy on yourself about others, such as fatty foods. Proponents of these diets suggest cutting back gradually to avoid this problem.

It certainly can help your overall health and sense of well-being to eat a balanced, sensible diet and to exercise often (see next section). A healthy diet, a good multivitamin and an exercise plan can make anyone feel better (and you probably know what's coming). Eat your fruits and vegetables. Cut back on fats and excessive carbohydrates. Replace refined flour with whole wheat wherever possible. Cut down on salt and sugar and reduced your caffeine intake. If you find that you get extremely irritable or weak and suddenly hungry when you haven't eaten in a while, you may be at least mildly hypoglycemic, so it may feel better if you eat meals that combine protein with complex carbohydrates, rather than something sugary. This may help reduce your craving for both sugar and alcohol. You may be surprised by how good a balanced diet and exercise can make you feel. Of course, individual results may vary. And I must recommend checking with your doc tor before starting any diet or exercise program, especially since symptoms of hypoglycemia can also indicate hyperglycemia (diabetes) and also hyperinsulinism.

PERSONAL FITNESS

As was briefly mentioned in the last section, exercise can play an important role in your recovery. It gives the body the feeling of health, supplies vital blood flow through the muscular system, promotes good sleep, improves bone density and releases those good endorphins in your brain, so that both your mind and body "feel right." Again, always check with your physician before starting any exercise program.

Physical exercise builds physical strength. With exercise, your muscles improve, your body tone improves and even your internal organs get stronger. Exercise builds mental strength as well, because it causes the body to produce endorphins, the body's natural tranquilizers and pain killers, which act on brain and nerve cells. They can calm you as powerfully as related chemicals such as morphine. Basically, endorphins create a natural "high." These strong biochemicals can help you beat depression and ward off anxiety.

David Appell, Director of Physical Fitness at Passages, states:

Ideally, you should exercise so that you are out of breath at least once a day-that is, breathing hard for at least five minutes. Jogging (even in place), exercising, or bike riding (either moving or stationary) will work. Having your body recover from getting out of breath becomes a rejuvenating experience where your physical systems work together- a concert of strengthening, stretching, hydration, nutrition and confidence. It also helps you develop increased functional movements and the ability to improve daily activities with a decrease in pain or discomfort.

Should you experience unusual pain, fainting or severe shortness of breath, stop and check with your doctor immediately.

Physical exercise not only helps build health and inner strength, it's one of the most powerful tools to help beat depression and anxiety. Aerobic exercise is a fast paced physical workout that lasts 20 to 30 minutes and it gives you the greatest production of endorphins. This type of exercise strengthens your heart and circulation and leaves you feeling relaxed for 12 to 24 hours. You will get the greatest benefits if you plan on three to four aerobic workouts a week. Studies have shown that the heart begins to lose the benefits of conditioning when more than two days go by without exercise.

It takes a while to break old patterns. Alcohol and drugs bring an instant high, without having to perform any activity. So give yourself time. Exercise brings about a natural "high", but it takes some time until you feel this benefit fully. The benefits, euphoria and relaxation, come gradually but are well worth it.

YOGA

Yoga is one of the most powerful relaxation techniques there is. It is a form of exercise based on the belief that the body and breath are intimately connected with the mind. By controlling the breath and holding the body in steady poses, yoga creates harmony. Yoga consists of many different stretching exercises, or poses, which you do in rhythm with your breathing. During the process of breathing as deeply as you can and moving as slowly as you breathe, your mind naturally focuses on the harmonious movement of body and breath and your blood is oxygenated while your heart rate becomes slow and steady.

Yoga is utilized to assist you to achieve balance and harmony of the body, mind and emotions. It helps you learn to withdraw from the chaos of the world and find a quiet space within. Yoga uses movement, breath, posture, relaxation and meditation in order to establish a healthy, vibrant and balanced approach to living. Often we use our addictions as a coping mechanism when we feel stressed. Rather than using drugs or alcohol as the solution for reducing stress, you can now use yoga, a superior tool not only to cope with stress but also change your state of consciousness in a manner that is not destructive to mind and body.

Several benefits of yoga include decreased stress levels, reduction of fatigue through savasana (relaxation), increased physical strength and flexibility and the flushing and removal of toxins through activating and stimulating circulation, digestion and elimination. Practicing yoga can also be an effective way of dealing with traumatic experiences that are often associated with drug and alcohol abuse. Yoga and meditation focus on removing stressful and distracting thoughts from your mind to help you regain composure and focus so you can successfully continue with your recovery. Learning to connect with pain and suffering (through yoga or meditation) creates the bridge to work towards self-love and healing, which can be a great motivator on the path to sobriety.

Moreover, yoga can actually alter brain neurology and help reduce cravings, anxiety and fear, all responses that can lead to destructive behaviors. Roy King, Ph.D. and M.D., an associate professor of psychiatry and behavioral science at Stanford University, has studied the biological impact of yoga on drug abuse. He explains that dopamine, a neurotransmitter, is elevated in the basal ganglia of the brain when drugs are introduced into the body. One physiological reason addicts go back for more is that their brain begins to crave that dopamine surge even when they just think about drug use. King explains that yoga and meditation may actually dampen dopamine activity in the basal ganglia, so that by inhibiting the dopamine impulse, yoga helps inhibit cravings and negative emotional states that trigger drug use. King also points out that some forms of yoga, like Kundalini which emphasizes intense breathing patterns, may actually trigger endorphins and activate the body's natural pleasure producer.

The idea of a yoga community can be a compelling notion for addicts. From a behavioral standpoint, a significant way to overcome temptation is just to stay away from people who use substances or from situations that cause anxiety. For addicts who often turn to abuse because they feel alienated, a yoga studio can offer a community of like minded people. Additionally, such a group has a greater potential for the cultivation of healthy friendships than would a bar or even an AA meeting.

NTR- NEUROTRANSMITTER RESTORATION

Drugs and alcohol have something in common: they both overstimulate certain neurotransmitter receptors (nerves) in the brain. This is how they bring about their effects, but it is also how they cause lasting damage that leads to deeper addiction and the inability to handle the stresses of normal life.

Developed by Dr. William Hitt over 20 years ago, neurotransmitter restoration system consists of a carefully designed intravenous solution of amino acids (the building blocks that make up all the proteins in our bodies) which actually rebuild the damaged areas of the brain. These amino acids are specifically formulated to be able to penetrate and positively influence the brain. By proving an abundant supply of the very amino acids needed to build new receptors, the cells are induced to switch gears and go into repair mode to fix what has been malfunctioning. The brain can then function again much more normally, cravings disappear, stress levels become much more normal and clarity of mind is restored. In other words, the NTR treatment is the process in which the brain's neurotransmitters are brought back into balance, allowing the brain to function as it did prior to the physical dependency on alcohol or other drugs.

As receptors are rebuilt and begin working again, cravings and drug tolerance rapidly decrease. NTR speeds up the physiologic brain recovery process to a mere ten days instead of weeks, months or even years it can take to repair cell damage caused by alcohol or drug use. While the effectiveness of NTR depends on the drug(s) used, the genetics of the patient's brain and how long the patient has been addicted, in general, more than 80% will achieve long-term abstinence, which is a 200%-700% increase in success rate than your typical program. NTR restores the body and brain *physically* from the damge done by drugs or alcohol. However, underling medical problems may still exist after treatment. These problems may include anxiety, depression, ADD and others. Getting addiction out of the way makes it possible to get at the causes of these other problems. It is important to understand that NTR eliminates physiologically based drug cravings but will have little impact upon the emotional or psychological components. So even if addiction is the sole problem, it would be advisable to receive continued psychological support for your long-term success in recovery, whether it's going to AA, seeing a therapist, individually or in a group, or simply joining a social group.

NTR is completely safe. The intravenous solutions are made from ingredients that occur naturally in the body and are prepared by a compounding pharmacy. Only FDA-approved ingredients of the highest purity are used. Dr. Hitt's work has been steadily gaining a reputation in addiction treatment as the most effective program in the world. Several clinics in the United States now offer the NTR System. (It was originally just available at the William Hitt Center in Tijuana, Mexico). If you are interested in more information, please visit his website, www.williamhittcenter.com, or call 888-671-9849. The treatment centers that use his approach in the U.S. that I found include NORA Clinic in Durango,

Colorado, ExecuCare addiction recovery center in Norcross, Georgia, Dr. Eli Ber, NMD in Scottsdale, Arizona, SouthCoast Recovery and Synergy Treatment in San Juan Capistrano, California, Turningpoint Clinic in Covington, Louisiana and NTR Hawaii in Honolulu, Hawaii.

AFFIRMATIONS

The most important addiction-treatment tool for your personal addiction recovery is YOU! This is for two reasons. First: only you can really motivate yourself. Second: all addictions are personal. So the place to make the most impact on your addictive behavior and potential recovery is within yourself; that is, your beliefs, your thinking, your feelings and your behaviors.

Affirmations are simply statements of positive truth. When we "do" affirmations, we take charge of that critical inner dialogue. By telling ourselves, "I am worthy even when I make a mistake," we legitimize that valid opinion whether or not we "feel" worthy at that moment. If we face ourselves in the mirror and say, "I am a lovable, competent, sober person," we might hear an inner voice saying, "Who are you kidding?" But just the verbal expression of the positive self-definition enters an authoritative new voice into the inner dialogue.

We are all internally compelled to behave or respond in any situation in a way that is consistent with our internalized self-concept. We originally developed our values and beliefs, which identify us to our selves, by what seemed to produce desirable results in our observed world. Some of our childhood survival strategies may no longer be valid in our adult world. We should probably just let them go.

Much of our behavior or action is determined non-consciously to support our personal values or ingrained beliefs, and we will go to all kinds of lengths to support those beliefs, including self-destructive behavior. We can, however, by effort and practice change our values and beliefs. This action on our part may be the most important step of our treatment. This is so vital because we behave in keeping with our self-concept. That is the way we have decided to define ourselves and the values and beliefs to which we subscribe. In other words, we can see ourselves as recovered, sober, serene, happy and productive members of society or see ourselves otherwise. It is our choice.

One way to help accomplish your goals and this change of attitude is through positive affirmations. Since repetition is the mother of habit change, your practicing of new behaviors can replace addictive behaviors with healthy ones. You can learn to give your subconscious mind the "OK" to alter your perceptions and therefore behaviors and in turn your life. Your non-conscious beliefs can be changed by your conscious mind just through the process of repeating positive affirmations which support your treatment values and recovery goals to which you aspire.

The longer and more often the affirmations are repeated, the higher priority they'll have in your belief system, and consequently the more the new recovery oriented values will influence your behavior. This practice allows your subconscious to act on the new values. The process is really quite simple in nature, however, it requires time, patience and persistence to accomplish. Your reward can be sobriety and a sense of serenity.

Here's the technique: Choose your affirmation, such as, "I choose not to drink", or "My body radiates health", or "I am strong," and repeat it over and over. Repeat it silently to yourself and repeat it out loud whenever you can. Also write out the entire affirmation over and over, 20 to 30 times at a sitting. Do this at least once a day. Then in time, weeks, not months or years, your new beliefs and behaviors can become congruent with your personal values.

SECTION III-FOR FAMILY MEMBERS AND OTHER LOVED ONES

What is important is to encourage the recovery method that your loved one has chosen for him or herself, regardless of your own beliefs. If this happens to be a 12-step program, you might want to try a 12-step program for yourself, such as Al-Alnon, to help you understand your loved one's situation better, and to deal with your own feelings and beliefs and problems in a safe and supportive setting. It is important that you take care of yourself first. If your emotional tank is running on empty, it is unlikely that you will be able to really help anyone else. If you have already begun to go to meetings, or are in any 12-step program yourself, you might insist to your loved one that there is no other way to get sober except through the 12 steps and they will otherwise fail. This is not a healthy attitude to take. Remember, AA and other 12-step programs are about attraction, rather than promotion. If you continue to insist, this might prevent your loved one from ever getting the help they need because there are many valid ways of recovery which may help, and if you tell them that the steps are the only way, they may reject them simply out of rebellion.

If they are refusing to take any action whatsoever to deal with their problem, you may need to distance yourself from them or take other measures you feel comfortable with. However, if they are honestly trying to get help and move forward, even if that means they have just cut down and are not completely abstinent, it's most likely best to be as supportive and encouraging as you can, whatever path your loved one decides to take. You need to be able to set limits but you also must have realistic expectations. How do you cope with frequent relapses or several failed treatment attempts? You have to keep in mind that severe addictions, often coupled with some sort of mental disorders, each carry a serious risk of fatal and near-fatal complications. Rather than looking for someone to blame, you need to remember that the person you love has a unique set of problems that can be chronic. The course is often quite rocky, and while many can and do improve, some may never recover. You may have to consider your loved one as though he or she had cancer: Treatment might help, permanent remission is possible, but death is always possible too. So stay in the present moment, rather than worrying about the future.

SECTION IV-WHAT WORKS? WHAT DOESN'T?

Reid Hester and William Miller have conducted the most exhaustive review of the treatment literature, and while they concluded that there was no single treatment that was superior to the others, they did find that individualizing treatment is crucial, and that there were many effective approaches available. Interestingly, some of the most effective treatments are the most difficult to find and the least well known, while the least effective are the most commonly used. As you will see, the list of least effective treatments will sound like the kind of care the majority of people with substance abuse problems now receive.

What Works:
Hester and Miller's Top Ten Alcohol Abuse Treatments with the Most Research Support

1. Brief interventions
2. Motivational-enhancement therapy- MET)
3. GABA agonist-Acamprosate (medication)
4. Community reinforcement approach
5. Self-help manual (CBT based)Behavior contracting (another behavioral approach)
6. Opiate antagonist-Naltrexone (medication)
7. Behavioral self-control training (another CBT approach)
8. Behavior contracting (CBT based)
9. Social-skills training (a type of cognitive and behavioral therapy- CBT)
10. Marital therapy-Behavioral

The treatments with the best research support are almost all cognitive/behavioral approaches. This means that rather than looking at substance abuse as a disease, it is something that is learned, and therefore, can be *un*learned. CBT is a nonconfrontational type of therapy that focuses on changing ones negative thoughts and behaviors, and by doing this, helping to prevent relapse. MET is designed to help people become motivated to quit or cut down on their drinking or drug use. It is the qualities of empathy and understanding that will determine the client's success. Clients are treated with respect, as an adult, not a child who needs to be yelled at. MET therapists will focus on a client's needs and goals and try to show them how their substance abuse is getting in the way of this. CBT is often used in conjunction with MET, which works to help people unlearn what substance abuse has taught them. The focus is on the thoughts and behaviors associated with the desire to drink or use and learning how to recognize them to avoid acting upon them. CBT has specific techniques and tools to change negative thinking that can lead to anxiety, depression and eventually relapse. When comparing CBT and MET to a 12-step approach, they are all about equally effective. When choosing a treatment, research shows that people do better when given a choice about their options. Therefore, you should go with the one that you feel most comfortable with.

What Doesn't Work
Hester and Miller's Bottom Ten Alcohol Abuse Treatments with the Least Research Support

1. Anxiolytic medication
2. Unspecified milieu therapy
3. Antidipsotropic-metronidazole (a medication)
4. Antidepressant medication (non-SSRI)
5. Videotape self-confrontation (usually using video to show people their bad behavior)
6. Relaxation training
7. Confrontational Counseling
8. Psychotherapy
9. General alcoholism counseling
10. Education (tapes, lectures, or films)

What's really interesting about this list is what is not readily seen. If I had listed the top 12 of the least effective treatments, you would have seen 12-step facilitation. The next one you would have seen is Alcoholics Anonymous. What was also found is that traditional psychotherapy is not useful in treating someone with a substance abuse problem, and that unless a person has received training in one of the effective techniques, such as CBT or MET, they are not going to be of much help. Unfortunately, most of the "professionals" at the traditional treatment centers are not required to get such credentials.

Now that you have an idea of what works and what doesn't, you will have more knowledge of the options that are now available and which one you feel will work best for you. You will also have a better understanding of what the treatment programs are offering. If you would like to see the complete list, it is available at www.behaviortherapy.com/whatworks.htm.

SECTION V- HOW TO CHOOSE A TREATMENT PROGRAM

How do you know what you are getting when you choose a rehab program? There are basically four types of programs:
- Moral
- Disease
- Behavioral
- Holistic

It is important to compare the different types of programs before making your decision. Many of them, especially in the U.S., are based on old ways of viewing the addicted person, and therefore their approach is often outdated.

In short, the *moral model* says that a person is bad if they make bad choices. (This was the main view before the disease model came into play in the 1930's.) The *disease model* views addiction like having a disease, akin to diabetes; the addicted person is completely powerless over their disease. The two models taken together offer a very bleak outlook. Addicts are bad people who have no control over their own lives. 12-step programs lean more toward the disease model. After these models, the *behavioral model*, or cognitive-behavioral model was developed. It says that each person has the power to change him or herself by changing the way they think. The newest model to emerge is the *holistic model*, which builds upon the good points of the older models. This approach uses the cognitive-behavioral model as a core component of its approach, and accounts for the many different contributing factors of the individual's unique addiction problem. This approach addresses the health of mind, body and spirit, helping the individual to both prevent and respond to their problems. It teaches self-management skills and techniques to prevent relapse and advocates a multi-faceted approach to support the individual. Most importantly, the holistic approach views individuals as competent to help themselves when given the right education, tools and support.

Let's look a bit deeper into the history and new developments in the addictions field, especially since addiction may be the most controversial topic that has been addressed in the public health and medical communities over the years. The addictions field has evolved through several phases over the past 100 years. What follows is a brief overview of some of the changes in belief regarding the basic nature of "addiction" or substance dependence, how to prevent its occurrence and how to intervene once dependence has become apparent. As shown above, addiction has been viewed as an individual moral problem, a medical disease and a behavioral disorder and now there's an emerging holistic model.

The Moral Model is the belief based on a moral theory. According to this theory, people are individually responsible for the behavioral choices they make, good or bad. Those who choose good behavior should be praised, while those who choose bad behavior need punishment. This leads to people with addiction problems to be stigmatized, labeling anyone with a "bad habit" as a "bad person." The downside of this model has become increasingly clear over the years. People with addiction problems are stigmatized and are therefore often demoralized by feelings of self-blame, guilt and shame to the extent that they are unwilling or unable to seek any help or treatment.

In the 1930's, the new Disease Model began to be formulated. This new view was that addiction was a disease caused by genetic and biological factors. The addict was then no longer held personally responsible for their 'bad behaviors" since these behaviors were now caused by biogenetic factors beyond their control. A strong argument could be made that addicts were patients deserving treatment, rather than criminals deserving punishment. The 12-step recovery movement with its accompanying treatment system enthusiastically accepted this model. Now, officially, addiction was a progressive disease for which there was no cure, and the only way to put the disease "in remission" was by a lifelong commitment to total abstinence. Any use of alcohol or other mind altering substances was considered a relapse, regardless if it resulted in any harmful consequences. So whether it was one drink or 100, it was treated the same.

Despite the wide acceptance and appeal of this disease model (over 90% of U.S. alcohol and drug treatment programs adhere to it), a number of shortcomings and limitations have emerged through years of research. Although these programs do work for some people, there are certain contradictions and paradoxes that prevent others from finding them helpful. The notion that the 12-step way of recovery is superior to all others is not at all backed by the research. People can recover without AA or any other 12-step program and be just as healthy as those who find them helpful. Within traditional treatment, there was a tendency toward a "one-size-fits-all" approach to recovery, which contributed to high dropout rates. And by defining addiction as an incurable, progressive disease, many people will find it difficult to change their addictive behaviors or decide to give up alcohol or drug use on their own.

In recent decades, an alternative model has emerged that challenges the traditional disease model and its "one-size-fits-all" approach to recovery. This model is based on the assumption that addictive behavior has multiple components and that individuals vary in risk depending on their unique bio-psycho-social history. Due to the fact that both habit acquisition and habit change are primarily influenced by cognitive and behavioral principles, this approach has become known as a cognitive-behavioral model. A major emphasis in this model is placed in the reward consequences of engaging in the addictive behavior, including both positive reinforcement, such as enhanced euphoria associated with getting high, and negative reinforcement, such as self-medication resulting in tension reduction or relief.

By bringing the attention back to the person with the substance abuse problem, treatment goals now shift from being strictly set by a treatment program provider, with abstinence as the only acceptable option, back to the consumer, (you), who now has a choice in their own treatment goals. Individuals can choose from a variety of goals, ranging from abstinence to reduction in harmful consequences, and by placing this choice into their hands, there is now acknowledgment that most addictive behaviors represent a problem in self-management that can be resolved by the individual. The substance abuser is no longer "powerless" but is taking back power over his or her own life. This model respects the client's choice and tries to meet clients where they are in the varying stages of behavioral change. This differs greatly from the traditional disease model, where emphasis is on client confrontation and enforcement of abstinence as the only acceptable goal.

The holistic model, or biopsychosocial model, is the emerging model, which takes a more holistic approach to health and well-being and incorporates the strengths of the various models of the past and uses those various insights to effect change. New understandings from years of research are coming into play and the holistic model is basing its approach on this important information. It is being discovered that social, economic, cultural and environmental conditions, as well as behavioral choices, impact both psychological and biological processes. In turn, psychological and biological changes influence behavioral patterns.

Now, motivational techniques, brief interventions, cognitive-behavioral therapy and pharmacotherapy co-exist with new approaches, including acupuncture, meditation, good nutrition and stress management (see previous section for more details). What has become clearer and clearer is the competence of individuals to manage their lives when information, support and choices are available.

Since the best predictor for your success is your ability to choose your own program and set your own goals, it is advisable to ask the following crucial questions to ensure that an appropriate drug and alcohol program is chosen that will meet your particular needs.

1. What kinds of treatment programs do they offer? Is it primarily 12-step based, or do they offer other self-help options as well, i.e. SMART Recovery, SOS, or Women For Sobriety? So they match treatment settings, interventions and services to each individuals particular problems and needs, since this is critical to one's ultimate success in returning to productive functioning in the family, workplace and society?
2. Does the program address multiple needs of the individual, not just his or her drug use, such as any associated medical, psychological, social, vocational and legal problems?
3. What types of credentials does the staff have, such as doctors, counselors, and anyone else who has contact with the clients, and what is the ratio between the staff and clients?
4. Is there a doctor on the treatment's premises 24 hours a day, or just a couple times a week to dole out medication?
5. What is the treatment program's philosophy or theory towards addiction? Is it religious, bio-psycho-social, psychological, neurological, physical and psychological, trauma-based (addiction that has stemmed from a sole traumatic event in one's life), and does their particular approach suit your own personality, beliefs and values, or is it one that you can believe in, and rebuild your life based on it?
6. Does the treatment program detail positive approaches towards

treatment, using up-to-date methods, such as motivational therapy, cognitive-behavioral therapy, stress personal responsibility, this is a disease/not a disease but a choice among many others?

7. Do you think this approach resonates with you, or your loved one, that may need inpatient help?

8. Does the program offer counseling (individual or group) and other behavioral therapies, where issues of motivation, building life-skills to resist drug and alcohol use, relapse prevention, improving problem-solving skills and facilitation of interpersonal relationships and ability to function in the family and community often take place?

9. How does the rehab program assist an individual during the withdrawal process, i.e. medical treatment for withdrawal provided, or must this be done somewhere else, prior to entering the facility?

10. To what extent is the family involved in the treatment process?

If a treatment program is determined to be necessary, asking these critical questions will at least give you the important information of whether or not they are simply a traditional treatment center, only offering one option, the 12-step method, or whether they have taken all the vital research into account and have now incorporated many different alternative modalities into their program. Remember, the notion that "one size fits all" in the treatment of alcohol and other drug problems has been completely destroyed by the scientific evidence, and therefore, there can not be a "one size fits all" solution.

SECTION VI-TO THE REHABS, SOBER LIVINGS, & OTHER INSTITUTIONS MANDATING 12-STEP PARTICIPATION LEGAL BASIS FOR EXPANDING KNOWLEDGE OF ALTERNATIVES-TREND FOR RECOVERY IN 21st CENTURY

Numerous cases, including *Griffin v. Coughlin* (New York, 1996), *Kerr v. Farrey* (7th Cir. 1996), *Arnold v. Tennessee Board of Paroles* (1997), *Warner v. Orange County Dep't of Probation* (2nd Cir. 1997), *Rauser v. Horn* (3rd Cir. 2001), and *Inouye v. Kemna et al* (9th Cir. 2007) are decided each year, ruling AA and other treatment programs based on AA's 12 steps "religious".

In all the cases, state agencies sentenced or otherwise compelled probationers or inmates to participate in such programs, which, according to the case decisions, violated the First Amendment's separation of church and state. In other words, it was *unconstitutional* to mandate participation in AA because it was found to be "unequivocally religious." (*Griffin v. Coughlin*). This was a landmark case that immediately affects all fifty states, in the sense that anyone can petition their state courts for declaratory relief from laws and regulations supporting mandated 12-step participation.

AA advocates have tried to state that their program is actually spiritual, *not* religious. One of AA's steps is to turn themselves over to a "higher power" as part of their recovery, but they state that the higher power can be anything, including a door knob! Whatever terminology AA wishes to use, courts disagree with their analysis and call a spade a spade, finding reference to God or a higher power in six of the 12 steps, to be, religious. The courts have also found that it is not only that most meetings begin and end with prayers, but that the fundamental nature of turning oneself over to a higher power is a religious concept.

So far, it appears that the two states that have been the most affected are California and New York. "In a 1994 case in federal court (*O'Connor vs. Orange County and the State of California*), AA was found to be "religious," and the State of California must now offer alternatives to 12-step programs in any state-funded or mandated program." (Trimpey, *AA: America's State Religion?*)

It has been made quite clear by the actions of New York's courts- the highest court in *Griffin v. Coughlin* and the federal appeals court in *Warner v. Orange County Dep't of Probation*- that state funded programs may not compel AA attendance. This ruling was extended even further in the 2nd Circuit appeals court in *DeStephano v. Emergency Housing Group et. Al* (2001). This court ruled that even though this program did not require clients to attend AA, the mere supervision of AA meetings by the program staff and reliance on AA literature was enough to be a violation of the First Amendment, and therefore, unconstitutional. "Based on *DeStefano*, New York's Office of Alcohol and Substance Abuse Services issued a bulletin to all government-funded providers stating that AA attendance could not be compulsory, treatment staff must not supervise AA meetings and programs could not require use of AA materials."

(Peele, *Is AA's loss psychology's gain?* 2004)

Over the past ten years, there has been a consistent trend in the courts to identify AA as religious, based on the content of the program and using *The Big Book and Twelve Steps* as exhibits, yet standard treatment programs, even in New York and California, have been slow to adopt the law laid out in *Warner* and *O'Connor*. This is because AA and the 12-step program are so ingrained in the American treatment protocol that many programs and counselors cannot even imagine alternatives. However, as I have previously mentioned, there *are* alternatives. "Eventually, a class action, a Supreme Court ruling, or both, will end the reign of the steps in America..." (Trimpey, *AA: America's State Religion?*) It is crucial that you are aware of the legal issues, and in light of these issues, it is imperative that you gain a better understanding of the alternative programs that are available.

CONCLUSION

It is my intention that this publication has given you a lot to think about, and more importantly, a lot of hope. Since its founding in the 1930s AA has helped many people overcome their dependency to alcohol and other drugs. Since it has been so helpful, many other offshoots of the program have been developed, such as NA and CA. For many people, however, viable options are desperately needed. As you can see, there are numerous alternatives to 12-step Programs. So whether you are having problems with the spiritual aspects of the 12-step program, you want to start taking responsibility and credit for your own life, you want a more positive program, or you simply have been in and out of AA for years, yet cannot seem to stay sober, I encourage you to take a look at some alternatives I have outlined to find out what resonates with you. Many of the Programs are not mutually exclusive with AA, or with each other. You now have more than one choice to form your own recovery plan; one that works for you, whether that results in being moderation or total abstinence. The days of, "*Get AA or die"* have now come to an end. It is about time since unfortunately, there have been way too many people who have come before you, taken that route with a tragic outcome.

While no one treatment approach has been proven more effective than another in *all* cases, particular approaches are more effective in *individual* cases. This is why it is so important to know about the alternatives that do exist, so that if one does not work for you, you can try another. Research is showing that if you are given a choice to pick the method that best suits you, and when you pick a goal, (abstinence or moderation), that you believe you can reach and maintain, you have a better chance for recovery, better than if you were forced to adhere to a particular method. In other words, "**You are more likely to succeed with a program that appeals to you personally; therefore, choosing a program you like is the best predictor for success.**" (Addiction Resource Center Inc.)

In our current system, many people are confronted with this dilemma: Either accept the 12-step model, even though you are not committed to it, nor may it be the most appropriate program for you, *or* be stigmatized as being "non-compliant" with treatment or "in denial." This labeling is commonplace in rehabs or sober living facilities where 12-step meetings are mandatory, and they are the *only* "treatment" offered. This will hopefully be a clue to rehabs, sober livings, and other institutions on how to best serve their clients in the future.

It should be noted that I have not covered *all* of the alternatives presently available. That is simply beyond the scope of this book. But for now, this is a beginning. If you have a problem, or know someone who does, please read this and spread the word! In our quest for freedom from addiction, we also need freedom of choice on the paths we take to get there.

Again… is the goal to get as many people into AA as we can, or is it to get them the help they really need? The choice is up to *us*… the individuals, the families, the therapists and psychiatrists, the rehabilitation centers, the sober livings, *and* the 12-step programs.

The next part of this book is devoted entirely to getting you the help you may want or need for yourself, or a loved one. In the next section, you will be able to find an individual, licensed professional in your area, who is registered either with SMART, who can provide moderation training or can offer cognitive behavior therapy. If you are unsure of what your goals are, meeting with one of these professionals can be a good place to start because they will be aware of the many alternatives available, and would be able to help you formulate what your next steps should be, i.e., whether a residential treatment program is necessary or desirable.

This is where the last part of this book comes in. It is a directory of treatment centers, both within the United States and abroad, which offer cutting-edge, scientific based alternatives to treatment. Some of the treatment facilities that are listed do still offer the traditional 12-step approach, but they are only listed here if they combine it with other treatment modalities as well. Others listed do not offer the 12-step approach at all. I have all of that information listed, as well as what kind of help is offered, i.e., detox, residential, outpatient, etc., in addition to the facilities' location and contact information. I hope this makes everything a little less overwhelming for you at this crucial time in your life.

Disclaimer: I do not endorse or oppose any of the recovery options mentioned in this book. I am simply supplying information about such groups. I am in no way affiliated with any of the following treatment programs, philosophies, methods, etc. and make no claim to be.

I do not recommend that anyone who has successfully maintained sobriety through one program should take it upon himself or herself to change treatment goals without first seeking professional assistance.

SECTION VII-LICENSED PROFESSIONALS

PART ONE: TREATMENT PROVIDERS REGISTERED WITH SMART

Note: The following have completed the registration form in Appendix G of the Coordinator's Manual. SMART Recovery® has made no effort to verify the accuracy of what these providers have reported to use. Nevertheless, they do report offering treatment that "is broadly based on the scientific findings on which SMART Recovery® is also based."

The reason I included this list is for people who might feel more comfortable working with someone, one-on-one, rather than going to meetings. Even though these providers are registered with SMART, it is likely that they can evaluate your individual situation and needs and be able to help you formulate a treatment plan using any number of alternatives. Even if you can not find a provider in your area, many can work with you over the phone.

CALIFORNIA:

Marc F. Kern, Ph.D. – (Los Angeles, CA)
Addiction Alternatives
Phone: (310) 275-LIFE, or (888) 22-HABIT
Email: habitdoc@gmail.com
Website: www.habitdoc.com

ILLINOIS:

Jean Alberti, Ph.D. – (Glen Ellyn, IL)
Phone: (630) 858-6977
Email: jalberti@mindspring.com

Doug Braun, MSW, CADS, MAC – (Naperville, IL)
Phone: (630) 548-2435
Email: Doug10767@aol.com

Douglas Culbert, Ph.D. – (Chicago & Evanston, IL)
Phone: (312) 467-1519
Email: d-culbert@uchicago.edu

Paul Fressola, LCSW, CADC – (Chicago, IL)
Phone: (773) 575-6323

Linda Goldsmith, LPC, CADC, OTR/L – (Highland Park & Evanston, IL)
Phone: (847) 477-3921
Email: LindaGoldsmith@mac.com
Website: www.goldsmithcounseling.com

Michael S. Shear, Psy.D. – (Peoria, IL)
Resolutions Unlimited
Phone: (309) 673-9385
Email: REBT2@mtco.com

MARYLAND:

Ralph D. Raphael, Ph.D.- (Baltimore, MD)
Phone: (410) 825-0042
Email: Ralph-raphael@erols.com

NEW JERSEY:

Jeffrey M. Brandler, EdS, CAS – (Mountain Lakes, NJ)
Phone: (973) 402-2647
Email: j.brandler@att.net
Website: www.changeispossible.org

Rich Dowling, LPC, MAC – (Morristown, NJ)
Phone: (973) 984-8244
Email: tte@thethoughtexchange.biz
Website: www.thethoughtexchange.biz

Martha M. Manger, MA, LPC, NCC, CCMHC- (Red Bank, NJ)
ProCounseling, LLC
Phone: (732) 741-0777
Email: Procounseling@optonline.net

Frederick Rotgers, Psy.D.- (Manasquan, NJ)
Phone: (215) 871-6457
Email: fred_etoh@yahoo.com

Margaret Tana, LPC, LCADC – (Kinnelon, NJ)
Phone: (973) 838-7265
Email: MAT6210@yahoo.com
Website: www.margaret-tana.com

NEW MEXICO:

John G. Gardin II, Ph.D. – (Albuquerque, NM)
John G. Gardin II and Associates
Phone: (505) 344-1776 ext 227, Cell/Pager: (505) 710-2871
Email: drjohngardin2@mac.com

Reid K. Hester, Ph.D. – (Albuquerque, NM)
Behavior Therapy Associates
Phone: (505) 345-6100
Email: rhester@behaviortherapy.com
Website: www.behaviortherapy.com

WISCONSIN:

Henry Steinberger, Ph.D. – (Madison, WI)
Alternative Recovery Options at Capital Associates, LLC
Phone: (608) 238-5176
Email: steinberger@sbcglobal.net

PART TWO: MODERATION MANAGEMENT-FRIENDLY PROFESSIONALS

Note: I obtained this list from the Moderation Management Network, Inc. (MM) provides this listing of moderation friendly therapists as a public service, and listing is at the request of the therapist. MM, and myself, make no guarantee about the competence of these therapists or the results you might achieve with them.

Even though these therapists are on a listed as "moderation management-friendly" therapists, it is likely that they could help you formulate a treatment plan using any of the alternatives listed in this book.

ARIZONA:

Robert Rhode, Ph.D. – (Tucson, AZ)
Phone: (520) 615-7623
Email: Rrhode@U.Arizona.edu

CALIFORNIA:

Christy Calame, LCSW – (Oakland, CA)
Phone: (510) 628-0877

Patt Denning, Ph.D. – (San Francisco, CA)
Harm Reduction Therapy Center
Phone: (415) 252-0669
Email: pdenning@harmreductiontherapy.org
Website: www.harmreductiontherapy.org

Mark F. Dolan, MFT – (Berkeley, CA)
Phone: (510) 848-4900 Office; (510) 932-9790 Cell
Email: mdolanmft@yahoo.com

Sam Garanzini, MA, MFT – (San Francisco, CA)
Phone: (415) 250-7642
Free Addiction Recovery Tips Newsletter:
www.samgaranzini.com/free_newsletter.php

Peter Goetz, MFT – (San Francisco and Emeryville, CA)
Phone: (415) 861-3816
Email: PeterGoetzMFT@aol.com
Note: Put "Moderation Management" in subject line

Valerie Gruber, Ph.D. – (San Francisco, CA)
UCSF Dep't of Psychiatry
Phone: (415) 502-5762

Sally Hand, Ph.D. – (San Francisco, CA)
Phone: (415) 337-4923

Arthur T. Horvath, Ph.D., ABPP – (La Jolla, CA)
Center for Cognitive Therapy
Phone: (858) 455-0042

Sean House, Ph.D. – (Palo Alto, CA)
Addiction Solutions Center
Phone: (650) 321-9300
Email: sean@addictionsolutionscenter.com
Website: www.addictionsolutionscenter.com

Phillip Keddy, Ph.D. – (Oakland, CA)
Phone: (510) 655-8824
Email: phillipkeddyphd@gmail.com
Website: www.drkeddy.com

Richard J. Kelliher, Psy.D. – (Santa Barbara, CA)
A Center for Cognitive Therapy
Phone: (805) 687-8021

Marc F. Kern, Ph.D. – (Los Angeles & Santa Ana, CA)
Addiction Alternatives-A Division of Life Management Skills, Inc.
Phone: (310) 275-5433; (714) 550-9311,
Email: habitdoc@gmail.com
Website: www.habitdoc.com

Laura M. Krum, Ph.D. – (San Francisco, CA)
Phone: (415) 509-3979
Email: lkrum@aol.com

Alesia Kunz, Ph.D. – (San Francisco, CA)
Phone: (415) 289-2018

Julie Leavitt, MD – (San Francisco, CA)
Available for both medication evaluations and therapy
Phone: (415) 550-7736

Jeannie Little, LCSW – (San Francisco, CA)
Phone: (415) 431-9848
Email: jlittle@harmreductiontherapy.org

Helen Marlo, Ph.D. – (Burlingame, CA)
Phone: (650) 579-4499

Gayle Paul, MFT – (San Francisco, CA)
Phone: (415) 586-5588 Office; (415) 412-9674 Cell
Email: GaylePaul@comcast.net
Website: www.gaylepaul.org

Practical Recovery Services – (La Jolla, CA)
Phone: (858) 453-4777
Email: info@practicalrecovery.com
Website: www.practicalrecovery.com

Sean P. Riley, Psy.D. – (San Francisco, CA)
Phone: (415) 948-4454
Email: drseanriley@yahoo.com
Website: www.drseanriley.com

Martha Stewart, MFT – (Orinda, CA)
Phone: (925) 254-8538
Email: marty@marthastewartmft.com

Dee-Dee Stout, MA, CADCII, SAP, MINT, ICADC – (San Francisco, CA)
Responsible Recovery
Phone: (510) 919-9678
Email: ddstoutrps@aol.com
Website: www.responsiblerecovery.org

Your Empowering Solutions, Inc. – (Rolling Hills Estates, CA)
Mary Ellen Barnes, Ph.D. President; Edward W. Wilson, Ph. D. Clinical Director
Phone: (888) 541-6350
Website: www.non12step.com

Adam Zimbardo, MFT – (San Francisco, CA)
Phone: (415) 280-2221
Email: adamzmft@mindspring.com
Website: www.adamzmft.net

COLORADO:

Chad Emrick, Ph.D. – (Aurora, CO)
A Clinic for Self-Management Inc.
Phone: (303) 290-0575

Diane Foss, MS – (Denver, CO)
Traditional and Alternative Therapy
The Renaissance Center
Phone: (303) 921-5125
Website: www.renaissancewellness.com

CONNECTICUT:

George H. Davis, Ph.D. – (New Haven, CT)
Phone: (203) 787-3070
Email: george.davis@snet.net

Georgette Wood, MA, LPC – (Branford, CT)
Phone: (203) 481-3757
Email: gwood@CreativeOptionsForLife.com
(Note: Put "Moderation Management" in subject line so not treated as spam)

DELAWARE:

Ron Wolskee, LCSW – (Newark, DE)
Counseling Services Inc.
Phone: (302) 894-1477
Website: http://ronwolskee.com/

DISTRICT of COLUMBIA:

Sima Stillings, MSW, LICSW, ACSW, MAC, SAP – (Washington, DC)
Harm Reduction Psychotherapy Institute
Phone: (202) 669-4413
Email: results@hrpi.org
Website: www.hrpi.org

FLORIDA:

Deborah A. Bruno, MSW, LCSW – (Miami, FL)
Phone: (305) 905-7177
Email: dbruno@caregiversolutionsfl.com

Ken Burg – (Ft. Lauderdale, FL)
Phone: (954) 920-3810
Email: kenburg@gte.net

Michael Dunn, Ph.D. – (Orlando, FL)
U. of Central Florida, Dep't of Psychology
Phone: (407) 823-3083
Email: mailtomdunn@pegasus.cc.ucf.edu

Linda Sobell, Ph.D. – (Fort Lauderdale, FL)
Guided Self-Change Clinic at Nova Southeastern University
Phone: (954) 262-5811

Email: sobelll@nova.edu or gsc@nova.edu
Website: www.nova.edu/gsc/

Mark Sobell, Ph.D. – (Fort Lauderdale, FL)
Guided Self Change Clinic
Center for Psychological Studies at Nova Southeastern University
Phone: (954) 262-5747
Email: sobellm@nova.edu
Website: www.nova.edu/gsc/

GEORGIA:

Maureen A. O'Harra, Ph.D. – (Decatur, GA)
Phone: (770) 270-5488
Email: maureenoharra@bellsouth.net

HAWAII:

Summer Eggleston, MFT, CSAC – (Kailua-Kona, HI)
Thought Field Therapy
Phone: (808) 327-1711

IDAHO:

Tony Cellucci, Ph.D. – (Pocatello, ID)
ISU Psychology Clinic
Phone: (208) 236-2129
Email: Cellanth@isu.edu

ILLINOIS:

Anne J. Buckingham, Ph.D. - (Chicago, IL)
Licensed Clinical Psychologist
Phone: (773) 334-5775

Vanessa E. Ford, LCSW, CADC – (Chicago, IL)
Phone: (773) 552-8070
Email: vanessaeford@gmail.com
Website: www.VanessaEFord.com

Paul Fressola, LCSW, CADC- (Chicago, IL)
Phone: (773) 575-6323

Scott R. Peterson, LCSW, CADC – (Chicago, IL)
Phone: (312) 515-3090
Email: srp1316@yahoo.com

Helen Redmond, LCSW, CADC – (Chicago, IL)
Phone: (312) 455-0999
Email: redmondmadrid@yahoo.com

Lisa J. Rivitz, LCSW, CADC – (Chicago, IL)
Phone: (773) 484-5186

INDIANA:

R. Lyle Cooper, Ph.D., LCSW, CADC – (New Albany, IN)
Associates in Counseling and Psychotherapy
Phone: (812) 944-1550
Email: LCooper@spalding.edu

LOUISIANA:

William C. Calkins, LCSW, BCD – (Baton Rouge, LA)
"One size does not fit all"
Phone: (225) 927-6444

David W. Earle, LPC – (Baton Rouge, LA)
Phone: (225) 293-3783

MARYLAND:

Jeffrey A. Schaler, Ph.D. – (Silver Spring, MD)
Phone: (202) 885-3667
Email: schaler@american.edu
Website: www.schaler.net

MASSACHUSETTS:

Dr. Mark Green, MD – (Cambridge, MA)
Phone: (617) 913-2971

Manfred J. Melcher, MSW, LICSW – (Easthampton, MA)
Phone: (413) 230-7131
Website: www.manfredmelcher.com

The Psychiatric Collaborative – (Orleans, MA)
Phone: (508) 240-7964
Email: priorco@aol.com

MINNESOTA:

James S. Anthony, Ph.D. – (White Bear Lake, MN)
Center for Human Development
Phone: (651) 426-8191
Website: http://spaces.msn.com/members/jsanthony/

Bruce Fischer, Ph.D. LP, LMFT – (Minneapolis, MN)
Core faculty Addiction Psychology Capella University
Phone: (612) 871-5829
Email: bfischer@capella.edu

Tamara J. Grams, LDAC – (St. Paul, MN)
AA Alternatives
Phone: (651) 645-6100
Website: www.aa-alternatives.com

MISSOURI:

Michelle Salois, MSW, RN, LCSW – (St. Louis, MO)
Clinical Member of American Association of Marriage & Family Therapy
Phone: (314) 993-8818
Email: michelsal@sbcglobal.net

NEBRASKA:

Lisa Obradovich – (Omaha, NE)
Therapy Solutions-Traditional and alternative CD treatment
Court mandated drug and alcohol classes
Phone: (402) 813-6673
Email: Lisa_OBradovich@msn.com

NEW JERSEY:

Susan Lynn Allen, MA, CADC – (Mendham, NJ)
Phone: (973) 543-5544

Jacqueline Bonanno, MA, LPC, CADC – (Morristown, NJ)
Phone: (973) 538-6353

Jeffrey M. Brandler, EdS, CAS – (Mountain Lakes, NJ)
Phone: (973) 402-2647

Michael Chenkin, LCSW, LCADC – (Somerville, NJ)
Phone: (732) 688-3493
Email: mchenkin_lcsw_lcadc@yahoo.com

Lorna Goldberg – (Englewood, NJ)
Phone: (201) 894-8515

Herb Goodfriend, LCSW, CADC – (Elizabeth, NJ)
Phone: (908) 351-6080

Raymond Hanbury, Ph.D. – (Manasquan, NJ)
Phone: (732) 223-1242

Julia Hough – (NJ)
Phoenix Rising Practitioner
Phone: (201) 558-1556
Email: juliahough@earthlink.net

Kevin J. Miller, Ph.D. – (Florham Park, NJ)
Phone: (973) 560-0595

Stanton Peele, Ph.D. – (Morristown, NJ)
Available in person, also for telephone consults and coaching
Phone: (973) 387-0475
Email: Stanton@peele.net
Website: www.peele.net

Frederick Rotgers, Psy.D. – (Manasquan, NJ)
Phone: (732) 528-0530
Email: fred_etoh@yahoo.com

Arnold M. Washton, Ph.D., & Assoc. – (Princeton, NJ)
Recovery Options
Phone: (609) 497-0433
Website: www.RecoveryOptions.us

NEW MEXICO:

Nancy Handmaker, Ph.D. – (Albuquerque, NM)
Behavior Therapy Associates, LLP
Phone: (505) 345-6100
Email: nhandmaker@behaviortherapy.com
Website: www.behaviortherapy.com

Reid K. Hester, Ph.D. – (Albuquerque, NM)
Behavior Therapy Associates
Phone: (505) 345-6100
Email: reidhester@behaviortherapy.com

Website: www.behaviortherapy.com www.drinkerscheckup.com (brief online motivation intervention for problem drinkers)

NEW YORK:

Carolyn Alroy, Psy.D – (New York, NY)
Phone: (212) 894-3710 Ext. 1269
Email: calroy@netscape.net

Patricia Bellucci, Ph.D. – (New York, NY)
St. Luke's/Roosevelt Hospital
Phone: (212) 787-3985

Deborah Birnbaum, Ph.D. – (New York, NY)
Phone: (212) 678-4758
Email: dbirnbaum@att.net

Genata Carol, Ph.D. – (New York, NY)
Phone: (212) 228-7154

Rachel Chernick, LCSW – (New York, NY)
Phone: (718) 541-1274 or (212) 523-6166
Email: rachelchernick@earthlink.net

Joanne De Rosa, LCSW – (New York, NY)
Phone: (212) 505-2258
Email: jdrcsw@aol.com

Charles Ehrhardt, MSW – (New York, NY)
Phone: (212) 677-7149
Email: cfehrhardt@aol.com

Fritz Galette, Ph.D. – (New York & Staten Island, NY)
Phone: (646) 265-2274

Stephen B. Goldman, Ph.D. – (New York, NY)
Phone: (212) 989-8528
Email: stephenbgoldmanphd@yahoo.com

William H. Gottdiener, Ph.D. – (New York, NY)
St. Luke's-Roosevelt Psychiatric Associates Faculty Practice
Phone: (212) 523-3996 Office; (917) 533-9124 Cell
Email: wgottdie@chpnet.org

Jack Herskovits, Psy.D. – (New York, NY)
Phone: (212) 924-3192

Nadia Jenefsky, LCAT – (Brooklyn, NY)
Phone: (917) 293-4642
Email: nadia@potentialspacenyc.com
Website: www.potentialspacenyc.com

Bruce Kellerhouse, Ph.D. – (New York, NY)
Phone: (212) 924-3293

Scott Kellogg, Ph.D. – (New York, NY)
The Cognitive Therapy Center of New York
Phone: (212) 221-1818
Email: kellogs@mail.rockefeller.edu

Ana Kosok, EdD – (New York, NY)
Telephone and email consultations available
Phone: (212) 781-3939
Email: AnaKosok@aol.com
Website: www.anakosok.com

Sari Kutch, CSW – (New York, NY)
Phone: (212) 561-1707
Email: sarigk@juno.com

Stephen A. Lisman, Ph.D. – (Johnson City, NY)
Susquehanna Psychological Affiliates
Phone: (607) 797-1652
Email: slisman@binghamton.edu

Camilla Mager, MA – (New York, NY)
Phone: (212) 696-6498

Gloria M. Miele, Ph.D. – (New York, NY)
Offers coaching
Phone: (212) 721-1880

Brian Murphy, LCSW – (New York, NY)
Available for face-to-face and telephone consultations
Phone: (917) 671-6923
Email: Murphy5554@aol.com
Website: www.selfledsolutions.com

Debra Rothschild, Ph.D., CASAC – (New York, NY)
Phone: (212) 721-1791

Lora Sassiela, CSW, BCD – (New York, NY)

Phone: (212) 844-0386

Dr. Mark Sehl – (New York, NY)
Available for face-to-face and telephone consultations
Phone: (212) 228-3467
Email: info@marksehl.com
Website: www.marksehl.com

Michelle Stocknoff, LMSW, CJAS – (New York, NY)
Phone: (917) 373-5131
Email: mstocknoff@hotmail.com

Andrew Tatarsky, Ph.D. – (New York, NY)
Phone: (212) 633-8157
Email: Atatarsky@aol.com
Website: www.andrewtatarsky.com

Deborah Washburn, LMSW – (New York, NY)
Phone: (917) 589-5603
Email: Washburndeborah@aol.com

Arnold M. Washton, Ph.D. & Associates – (New York, NY)
Recovery Options
Phone: (212) 944-8444
Website: www.RecoveryOptions.us

Carrie Wilkens – (New York, NY)
Center for Motivation and Change
Phone: (212) 683-3339
Email: cwilkens@motivationandchange.com
Website: www.motivationandchange.com

NORTH CAROLINA:

R. Trent Codd, III, LPC, ACT, CCAS – (Asheville, NC)
Cognitive-Behavioral Therapy Center of WNC, P.A.
Phone: (828) 350-1177
Email: rtcodd@behaviortherapist.com
Website: www.behaviortherapist.com

Mark D. Worthen, Psy.D., CCAS – (Charlotte, NC)
Phone: (704) 347-8862
Website: www.drworthen.com

OHIO:

Harold Rosenberg – (Bowling Green, OH)
Psychology Dep't-Bowling Green State University
Phone: (419) 372-2540
Email: hrosenb@bgnet.bgsu.edu

SOUTH CAROLINA:

Linda Scott, CACII, LPC – (Mt. Pleasant, SC)
Phone: (843) 884-3070
Email: LScottcounseling@comcast.net
Website: www.lscotttherapy.com

Gretchen Sparacino, MA, LPC – (James Island, SC)
Phone: (843) 475-6447

TEXAS:

William J. Dubin, Ph.D. – (Austin, TX)
Psychological Assessment Research and Treatment Services
Phone: (512) 343-8307
Email: bill@psycharts.com

Paul S. Silver, Ph.D. – (Dallas, TX)
Phone: (214) 373-9631

WASHINGTON:

Amy Summers, Ph.D. – (Seattle, WA)
Phone: (206) 522-4104
Website: www.amysummersphd.com

Pioneer Human Services – (Seattle, WA)
The Augustine Clinic- Contact Tarolyn Burke
Phone: (253) 222-3449
Email: coach@enrichedlivingcoaching.com

WISCONSIN:

Edward M. Rubin, Psy.D. – (Milwaukee, WI)
Behavioral Health Services
Phone: (414) 219-5135
Email: erubin@facstaff.wisc.edu

Henry Steinberger, Ph.D. – (Madison, WI)
Capital Associates, LLC
Phone: (608) 238-5176
Email: steinberger@sbcglobal.net

Providers of Alcohol Management Program Training (see Alcohol Management Program in next section):

Donna Dotson – (Ann Arbor, MI)
University of Michigan Hospital

Chad Emrick, Ph.D. – (Aurora, CO)
A Clinic for Self-Management Inc.
Phone: (303) 290-0575

Jim Goldman – (Iowa City, IA)
Manager Faculty, EAP at University of Iowa
Email: jim-goldman@uiowa.edu

Daryl Minicucci – (Manlius, NY)
Phone: (315) 682-9825

PART THREE: COGNITIVE BEHAVIORAL THERAPISTS

Note: I obtained this list of therapists from both the Albert Ellis Institute, who are trained in Rational Emotive Behavioral Therapy (REBT), and the National Association of Cognitive Behavioral Therapists (NACBT). I make no guarantee about the competency of these therapists or the results you might achieve with them. The reason I included them was because of Hester and Miller's study, (which was discussed in the section "What Works? What Doesn't?") In their exhaustive review, cognitive behavioral therapy was cited various times as to what was the most effective modality in their top ten alcohol abuse treatments. Most of the therapists listed deal with addictions as well as other issues, such as co-occurring disorders, stress management, coping skills, PTSD, etc. I was able to include a brief synopsis of some of the NACBT's specialties since they provided that information on their website, (this information was not available on the Albert Ellis website) so it is ultimately up to you to call and find out what all of their specialties are, and if they match your specific needs. (If there is not one in your area, try to find one that will work with you over the phone. If you would like more information, go to www.rebt.org/referral_list for the Albert Ellis Institute therapists and http://nacbt.org/searchfortherapists.asp for the National Association of Cognitive Behavioral Therapists.

ALABAMA:

Danny E. Blanchard, Ph.D., PC – (Huntsville, AL)
Counseling Associates
Alcohol abuse, ADD/ADHD, depression, obsessive-compulsive disorder, stress management
Phone: (256) 895-6617
Email: blanchadn@bellsouth.net
Website: www.marriagefamilyservices.com

Katherine Helm-Hinton, MSW – (Tuscaloosa, AL)
Addictive behavior, anxiety, bipolar, depression, coping skills, stress management, trauma
Phone: (205) 310-2650

Michael S. Rosenbaum, Ph.D. – (Mobile, AL)
Addictive behavior, adolescent issues, anxiety, bipolar, depression, eating disorders, parenting and stress management
Phone: (251) 344-1482
Email: drmsr@bellsouth.net

Fred P. Stone, Ph.D. – (Maxwell, AL)
Phone: (334) 239-8192
Email: fsstone@hotmail.com

ARKANSAS:

Michael Forrest, Ed.D, LPC, LMFT – (Rogers, AR)
ADD/ADHD, anxiety, depression, coping skills, stress management, trauma
Phone: (479) 631-2658
Email: mforrestedd@att.net

ARIZONA:

Marie A. Brangenberg, MA – (Tucson, AZ)
Casa Church Womens Ministries
Anxiety, coping skills, panic disorders, PTSD, stress management, trauma
Phone: (520) 878-1106
Email: jmbrangenberg@msn.com

Linda Cohn, Ph.D. – (Scottsdale, AZ)
Addictive behavior, ADD/ADHD, adolescent issues, anxiety, biofeedback, coping
skills, hypnosis, pain management, PTSD
Phone: (480) 941-4466
Email: Drlcohn01@aol.com

James P. Krehbiel, Ed.S – (Scottsdale, AZ)
Adolescent issues, anxiety, depression, obsessive-compulsive disorder, PTSD,
social skills training
Phone: (480) 664-6665
Email: jkboardroomsuites@yahoo.com

Dr. Rick Merrell, Ph.D. – (Winslow, AZ)
Addictive behavior, AIDS/HIV infection, anxiety, coping skills, depression, social
skills training
Phone: (928) 289-0500
Email: ctimagape@yahoo.com

Ky S. Resh, MSW – (Tucson, AZ)
Addictive behavior, adolescent issues, anxiety, depression, obesity, trauma
Phone: (520) 320-9996
Email: chisresh@msn.com

CALIFORNIA:

Alan H. Berkowitz, Ph.D. – (Calabasas, CA)
Phone: (818) 223-8670
Email: DrAlan49@gmail.com

Karen Cohen, LMFT, CGP – (Sherman Oaks & Glendale, CA)
Addictive behavior, adolescent issues, anxiety, bipolar, eating disorders, PTSD,

stress management
Phone: (818) 400-1001
Email: kcmft88@yahoo.com

Dr. Michael R. Edelstein, Ph.D. – (San Francisco, CA)
Addictive behavior, adolescent issues, anxiety, depression, eating disorders,
obsessive-compulsive disorder, PTSD, sleep disorders
Phone: (415) 673-2848
Email: DrEdelstein@ThreeMinuteTherapy.com
Website: www.ThreeMinuteTherapy.com

Charles A. Hogan, Ph.D. – (Chula Vista, CA)
Phone; (619) 656-3775
Email: Charles.Hogan@gmail.com

Vicki Joseph, MSW – (Vacaville, CA)
Addictive behavior, anxiety, bipolar, depression, obsessive-compulsive disorder,
social skills training, trauma
Phone: (513) 405-1643
Email: vj0@comcast.net

Ronald Ober, LCSW – (Hollister, CA)
Addictive behavior, ADD/ADHD, adolescent issues, anxiety, bipolar, coping
skills, depression, trauma
Phone: (831) 637-6787
Email: rsober@charter.net

David M. Pittle, Ph.D. – (San Rafael, CA)
Anxiety, bipolar, coping skills, depression, hypnosis, obsessive-compulsive
disorder, pain management, smoking addiction
Phone: (415) 479-3945
Email: davidpittle@turningspirit.com
Website: www.turningspirit.com

Enid Richey, Ph.D. – (Rancho Cucamonga, CA)
Addictive behavior, anxiety, bipolar, depression, PTSD, rape, trauma
Phone: (909) 980-3567

Roberto G. Romandia, MS, LEP, CCBT – (Porterville, CA)
Adolescent issues, alcohol abuse, anxiety, coping skills, depression, PTSD,
social skills training
Phone: (559) 920-2350
Email: excalbur@charter.net

Doris R. Sami, DSW, LCSW – (Santa Rosa, CA)
Adolescent issues, ADD/ADHD, anxiety, bipolar, eating disorders, social skills

training
Email: doris@sami.org
Website: http://sami.org

COLORADO:

Dr. Laurie Berger-Jackson, Ph.D. – (Littleton & Aurora, CO)
Addictive behavior, anxiety, bipolar, EMDR, eating disorders, PTSD, sleep disorders, trauma
Phone: (720) 312-8691
Email: centurycontractors@msn.com

Margie Dudley, MA – (Colorado Springs, CO)
Addictive behavior, anger, anxiety, bipolar, eating disorders, sexual behavior
Phone: (719) 473-1805

Dr. Lisa C. Holder – (Colorado Springs, CO)
Addictive behavior, ADD/ADHD, adolescent issues, anxiety, biofeedback, coping skills, depression, eating disorders, pain management
Phone: (719) 630-0222
Email: lisa@mindbodytech.com

Zach Nelson – (Pagosa Springs, CO)
Addictive behavior, ADD/ADHD, anxiety, depression, PTSD, stress management
Phone: (970) 422-4143
Email: Zachariah@skywerx.com

CONNECTICUT:

Patricia A. Bailey, MC, NCC, LPC – (Danbury, CT)
Ct. Labor Dept
Coping skills, PTSD, rape, social skills training, stress management
Phone: (203) 797-4151

Domiic Dimatta, Ed.D – (Goshen, CT)
Phone: (860) 491-1057
Email: domrebt@hotmail.com

Mike Friedman, Ph.D. – (New London, CT)
New London Counseling
Addiction behavior, ADD/ADHD, anxiety, biofeedback, bipolar, EMDR, hypnosis, PTSD, sleep disorders, stress management
Phone: (860) 447-9935

Steve A. Johnson – (Avon, CT)
Valley Community Baptist Church

Phone: (860) 673-6826
Email: stjohnson@valleycommunity.cc

Janet M. Schwenger, Ph.D. – (Hamden, CT)
Behavioral Health Consultants
REBT , anxiety, depression, anger management, bipolar, eating disorders
Phone: (203) 288-3554 x24; (203) 582-3824
Email: jschwenger@sbcglobal.net

DISTRICT OF COLUMBIA:

Larry Cohen, LICSW, DCBT – (Washington, D.C.)
Addictive behavior, AIDS/HIV infection, anxiety, depression, social skills training
Phone: (202) 244-0903
Email: larrycohen@socialanxietyhelp.com
Website: www.socialanxietyhelp.com

Dr. Carolyn E. Gravely-Muss, LPC, CBT, LSW – (Washington, D.C.)
Crisis Management Intrespect
Adolescent issues, anxiety, biofeedback, coping skills, hypnosis, PTSD, obsessive-compulsive disorder, psychopharmacology
Phone: (202) 581-0778
Email: cegm1448@verizon.net

Vincent Greenwood, Ph.D. – (Washington, D.C.)
Depression, anxiety disorders
Phone; (202) 244-0260
Email: vgwcct@aol.com

FLORIDA:

Dr. Barry Arnold, MDiv, Ph.D. – (Milton, FL)
Christian Clinical Counseling
Coping skills, aging, pre-marital therapy, religious issues
Phone: (850) 626-4560
Email: Cclinical@mchsi.com

Amelia Binda, Ph.D. – (Clearwater & Tampa, FL)
Phone: (727) 686-4357

Harold Bishop, LCSW, CAP – (Dunedin & St. Petersburg, FL)
Phone: (727) 347-3284
Email: halbfla@verizon.net

Lynda E. Bolt, MA – (Ft. Walton Beach, FL)
Addictive behavior, adolescent issues, anxiety, bipolar, depression, eating

disorders, stress management, pain management, PTSD
Phone: (850) 243-7035

Neysa Buckle, MS – (Sarasota, FL)
Mindspa
Addictive behavior, anxiety, biofeedback, bipolar, depression, eating disorders,
PTSD, stress management, trauma
Phone: (941) 448-4931
Email: naace@behaviorcoach.org
Website: www.behaviorcoach.org

Bert Diament, Ph.D. – (Palm Beach Gardens, FL)
Phone: (561) 629-2211
Email: bdphd@comcast.net

Robert (Ruben) Drake, MA – (Tampa, FL)
Columbus juvenile residential facility
Phone; (813) 769-0445 x104
Email: rdrake@sunshineys.net
Website: www.sunshineservices.com

Michael Dubi, Ed.D., LMHC – (Port Charlotte, FL)
Addictive behavior, adolescent issues, AIDS/HIV infection, anxiety, biofeedback,
depression, EMDR, hypnosis, PTSD, sexual behavior
Phone: (941) 724-1026
Email: mdubi@comcast.net

Jill Foxman, Ph.D., LMAC – (Delray Beach, FL)
Fox Counseling
Addictive behavior, ADD/ADHD, anxiety, bipolar, depression, eating disorders,
social skills training, stress management
Phone: (561) 274-3943
Email: jfx97@aol.com
Website: www.psychologytoday.com

Caryn L. Goldberg, Ph.D. – (Delray Beach, FL)
Healthy Insights, Inc.
Anxiety, bipolar, coping skills, depression, stress management
Phone: (561) 498-8585
Email: Goldberg_c@bellsouth.net
Website: www.healthyinsights.com

Whitford-Thomas Group, Inc. – (Tampa, FL)
David L. Thomas, Ph.D., LMHC
Robert W. Whitford, Ed.S., LMHC
Phone: (813) 872-8022

Email: david@whitfordthomasgroup.com, bob@whitfordthomasgroup.com

Dr. John M. Gullo, Ed.D. – (Tampa, FL)
Psychotherapy & Hypnotherapy
Phone: (813) 961-5859
Email: drjgullo@aol.com

Robert F. Heller, Ed.D. – (Boca Raton, FL)
Anxiety, depression, anger, addictions & performance issues
Phone: (561) 451-2731
Email: rheller2007@comcast.net
Website: www.robertheller.net

Jody L. Kaler, Ed.S. – (Stuart, FL)
Kaler Psychotherapy
Addictive behavior, ADD/ADHD, adolescent issues, bipolar, depression, obesity, PTSD, sleep disorders
Phone: (772) 287-3780

Dulce M. Matamoros, Ph.D. – (Hialeah, FL)
Adolescent issues, ADD/ADHD, bipolar, coping skills, depression, PTSD, psychopharmacology, social skills training
Phone: (786) 306-3397
Email: srassha1@bellsouth.net
Website: www.psyfl.tripod.com

Lee A. Wilkinson, Ph.D. NCSP – (Jupiter, FL)
ADD/ADHD, autism, social skills training, adolescents
Phone: (561) 745-7261

John Yurick, Ph.D. – (Longwood, FL)
Phone: (407) 830-9599

GEORGIA:

Karen Greene, LPC, LMFT – (Marietta, GA)
Anxiety, coping skills, depression, obsessive-compulsive disorder, social skills training, stress management
Phone: (770) 973-8208
Email: Kgreene3333@aol.com

Dr. Kathy Howell, LPC, Ph.D. – (Dowsonville, GA)
Accares
Addictive behavior, ADD/ADHD, adolescent issues, anxiety, bipolar, depression, eating disorders, pain management, PTSD, stress management
Phone: (706) 216-6356

Email: AccaresDKH@windstream.net

Dr. Stephen M. Mathis, Psy.D. – (Roswell, GA)
Applied Psychology Associates
Addictive behavior, ADD/ADHD, adolescent issues, anxiety, coping skills,
depression, eating disorders, EMDR, hypnosis, PTSD, social skills training
Phone: (770) 645-1800
Email: smm3@windstream.net
Website: www.psychdoc.com

Joan Miller, Ph.D. – (Marietta, GA)
Addictive behavior, anger, anxiety, couples counseling, depression, divorce
counseling, smoking cessation, stress management
Phone: (770) 952-3308
Email: joanmiller@mindspring.com
Website: www.JoanMillerPhD.com

HAWAII:

Jerry M. Brennan, Ph.D. – (Honolulu, HI)
Addictive behavior, anxiety, bipolar, coping skills, depression, eating disorders,
PTSD, stress management, trauma
Phone: (808) 538-0343
Email: jb@jerrymbrennan.com
Website: www.jerrybrennan.com

Stann W. Reiziss, Ph.D. – (Kailua-Oahu, HI)
Hypnosis and Counseling Information and Referral
Addictive behavior, ADD/ADHD, adolescent issues, anxiety, coping skills,
depression, hypnosis, obesity, pain management, PTSD, trauma
Phone: (808) 261-2618
Email: reiziss@hawaiiantel.net
Website: www.drhypnos.info

IOWA:

Toni R. Bell, MA – (Windsor Heights, IA)
Counseling for Growth and Change
Addictive behavior, adolescent issues, anxiety, coping skills, depression, pain
management, PTSD, rape, stress management, trauma
Phone: (515) 243-1020
Email: trbell@mcleodusa.net
Website: www.counselingforgrowthandchange.com

Larry L. Koch, MA – (Des Moines, IA)
Anxiety, bipolar, depression, obsessive-compulsive, psychopharmacology

Phone: (515) 282-6919
Email: lkoch@broadlawns.org

ILLINOIS:

Leon B. Black, MSW, LCSW – (Rockford, IL)
Leon Black Counseling Services
Adolescent issues, depression, panic disorders, PTSD, religious issues
Phone: (815) 398-7000
Email: lblack9262@aol.com

Chicago Institute for REBT – (Chicago, IL)
Terry London, M.S.
Paul Hauck, Ph.D.
Phone: (847) 952-0150
Email: mapah53@mchsi.com

Deborah R. Gholsom – (Ashley, IL)
Shiloh Partners in Health
Adolescent issues, ADD/ADHD, anxiety, depression, coping skills, PTSD, sexual behavior, sleep disorders, social skills training, stress management
Phone: (618) 246-6075
Email: debcec@americonnect.net

David C. Penn, Ph.D. – (Robbins, IL)
Imani Counseling Services
Adolescent issues, religious issues, school psychology, education and teaching
Phone: (708) 466-2145
Email: kennedy/23@aol.com

Michael S. Shear, Psy.D. – (Peoria, IL)
Phone: (309) 673-9385
Email: REBT2@mtco.com

INDIANA:

Mr. Stephen T. Gregg – (Indianapolis, IN)
S.T. Gregg and Associates
Addictive behavior, anxiety, coping skills, PTSD, social skills training, stress management
Phone: (317) 823-9605
Email: N9RKS@ARRL.net

James Christopher Plew, MS (Indianapolis, IN)
J. Christopher Plew, Inc.
Anxiety, ADD/ADHD, coping skills, depression, obsessive-compulsive, PTSD,

sexual behavior, social skills training
Phone: (317) 304-6022
Email: jchrisplew@aol.com

Jeanette Walton, LCSW – (Greenfield, IN)
Ecolife Advantage
Adolescent issues, ADD/ADHD, anxiety, biofeedback, coping skills, depression, eating disorders, pain management, PTSD, sleep disorders, social skills training
Phone: (317) 462-2665
Email: Dr.J.Walton@sbcglobal.net

KANSAS:

Harriet H. Barrish, Ph.D. – (Leawood, KS)
Phone: (913) 491-4343

Arthur D. McKenna, Ph.D. – (Topeka, KS)
Phone: (785) 273-8574

KENTUCKY:

Richard Applegate, MA – (Elizabethtown, KY)
Lincoln Village
Phone: (270) 766-5283 x233
Email: Richard.Applegate@ky.gov

Donald Beal, Ph.D. – (Richmond, KY)
Eastern Kentucky University, Department of Psychology
Phone: (859) 622-1108
Email: Don.Beal@Eku.edu

Dr. Rick Roepke, CCBT – (Bowling Green, KY)
Christian Family Institute/Roepke and Roepke, LLC
Anxiety, coping skills, depression, obesity, PTSD, religious issues, social skills training, stress management, trauma
Phone: (270) 746-0283
Email: cficareky@aol.com
Website: www.christianinstitute.net

LOUISIANA:

Mark S. DeBord, LCSW – (West Monroe, LA)
First West Counseling Center
Anxiety, coping skills, depression, PTSD, religious issues, social skills training
Phone: (318) 322-1427; (318) 381-9070
Email: msdebord@comcast.net

Jacqueline Mims, Ed.D., Ph.D. – (Baton Rouge, LA)
Eclectic Rehabilitation Counseling Services, LLC
Adolescent issues, ADD/ADHD, anxiety, coping skills, depression, PTSD, rape, religious issues, social skills training, violence
Phone: (225) 357-5171

MAINE:

Catharine MacLaren, LCSW – (Portland, ME)
Phone: (207) 899-6175
Email: maclarenc@aol.com

MASSACHUSETTS:

Ken Barringer, MA – (Newton, MA)
The Academy
Adolescent issues, ADD/ADHD, anxiety, coping skills, depression, parenting, social skills training
Phone: (817) 969-2200 x12
Email: kbarringer@comcast.net
Website: www.academy.com

Janine Gendreau, MA – (Fall River, MA)
Arbour Counseling Services
Addictive behavior, ADD/ADHD, adolescent issues, AIDS/HIV infection, anxiety, bipolar, depression, coping skills, obesity, PTSD, rape, religious issues
Phone: (508) 678-2833
Email: janinegendreau@yahoo.com

Herman Lowe, Ph.D. – (Newton & Plymouth, MA)
Phone: (617) 510-6379; (508) 830-0397
Email: hermanlowe@comcast.net

Chippa Martin, MA – (Brookline, MA)
Adolescent issues, alcohol abuse, anxiety, coping skills, eating disorders, PTSD, rape, social skills training, stress management
Phone: (617) 244-4557

Maria Vastis Saxionis, MSW – (Ashland, MA)
Alpha Counseling and Consultation
Addictive behavior, adolescent issues, AIDS/HIV infection, anxiety, depression, eating disorders, parenting, PTSD, psychopharmacology, rape, sexual behavior
Phone: (508) 881-2860
Email: msaxionis@msn.com

Cara Vecchio, Ph.D. – (Newburyport, MA)
Work-related stress, anxiety, anger management
Phone: (978) 270-8268
Email: Cvecchio1@yahoo.com

MARYLAND:

Donna E. Burns, LCPC, CCBT – (Baltimore, MD)
Anxiety, obsessive-compulsive, phobias, social anxiety
Phone: (410) 938-8464

Christopher W. Shea, MA, CRAT – (Havre de Grace, MD)
Addictive behavior, anxiety, coping skills, religious issues, stress management
Phone: (410) 409-9164
Email: chrismd104@yahoo.com

MICHIGAN:

Thomas F. Mooney, Ed.D. – (Port Huron, MI)
Phone: (810) 982-2313
Email: 9234@sbcglobal.net

William Nash, MA (Madison Heights, MI)
Addictive behavior, depression, religious needs
Phone: (248) 967-7290

Delbert Teachout, Ph.D. – (Wyoming, MI)
Addictive behavior, religious issues
Phone: (616) 406-1850
Email: teachout_delbert@sbcglobal.net

MISSOURI:

David J. McWilliams, ME.d. – (Kansas City, MO)
MO Dept of Mental Health
Addictive behavior, adolescent issues, anxiety, coping skills, obsessive-compulsive, psychopharmacology, social skills training, stress management
Phone: (816) 482-5777
Email: david.mcwilliams@dmh.mo.gov

NEVADA:

Dr. Robert D. Smyly, Psy.D. – (Reno, NV)
Successful Transitions

Addictive behavior, AIDS/HIV infection, coping skills, employee assistance, sexual behavior, social skills training, stress management
Phone: (775) 770-2242
Email: successfultrnstns@sbcglobal.net

NEW HAMPSHIRE:

Joanne Groetzinger, MS, MA – (Barrington, NH)
Bridging Lives Together
Adolescent issues, ADD/ADHD, AIDS/HIV infection, anxiety, bipolar, coping skills, depression, PTSD, social skills training, stress management
Phone: (603) 608-8485
Email: jogblt@aol.com

NEW JERSEY:

Lidia D. Abrams, Ph.D. – (Clifton & Jersey City, NJ)
Mike Abrams, Ph.D.
Phone: (973) 742-3113; (201) 653-5222
Email: lidpsy@aol.com

Rich Dowling, MA, LPC, MAC – (Morristown, NJ)
The Thought Exchange
Phone: (973) 984-8244
Email: tte@thethoughtexchange.biz

Dr. Eli M.S. Forman, Ph.D. – (Leonia, NJ)
DBK Dr. Eli M.S. Forman
Addictive behavior, adolescent issues, anxiety, depression, coping skills, eating disorders, hypnosis, PTSD, sexual behavior, stress management
Phone: (201) 592-7388
Email: DrEliLeoniaNJ@aol.com

Dr. Dennis L. Gilliams, Ph.D. – (Maple Shade, NJ)
Addictive behavior, ADD/ADHD, adolescent issues, AIDS/HIV infection, anxiety, bipolar, coping skills, depression, hypnosis, sexual behavior
Phone: (856) 321-5588
Email: ctzn56@msn.com

Judith Green, Ph.D. – (Teaneck, NJ)
Phone: (201) 315-9876
Email: jugreen@optonline.net

Marion Hecht – (South Orange, NJ)
Addictive behavior, ADD/ADHD, adolescent issues, anxiety, depression, coping skills, eating disorders, PTSD, social skills training, stress management, trauma

Phone: (973) 762-1224

Jean Heindl, MSW - (Phillipsburg, NJ)
Adolescent issues, anxiety, depression, coping skills, hypnosis, obesity, PTSD, religious issues, sexual behavior, social skills training, stress management
Phone: (908) 213-8944
Email: jean.heindl@affiliatescs.com

Alfred Hurley Jr., Ph.D. – (Haworth, NJ)
Children & adolescents
Phone: (201) 385-6248
Email: uxmal40@aol.com

Robert C. Kornhaber, Ph.D. – (Fort Lee & Milburn, NJ)
Panic Disorder, phobias, depression, & couples counseling
Phone: (201) 944-3665; (973) 376-6062

Arnold A. Lazarus, Ph.D. – (Princeton, NJ)
Phone: (609) 924-8450
Email: aalaz@aol.com

Stuart M. Leeds, Psy.D. – (Parsippany, NJ)
Morris Psychological Group
Phone: (973) 257-9000 x24
Email: drstu@morrispsych.com

John F. McInerney, Ph.D. – (Cape May Court House, NJ)
Cape Behavioral Health Group
Children & adolescents, addictive disorder, alcohol dependencies
Phone: (609) 463-1662
Email: jfmcin@comcast.net

James McMahon, Psy.D., Ph.D. – (Island Heights & Westfield, NJ)
Phone: (732) 684-0524
Email: bjpsymac@msn.com

Dante C. Mercurio, Ph.D. – (West Caldwell, NJ)
Phone: (973) 227-0642
Email: dmerc@verizon.net

Marilyn Oldman, Ed.D. – (Watchung, NJ)
Individual, group, couples therapy, women's issues, parenting counseling
Phone: (908) 753-9797
Email: marilynoldman@aol.com

Joseph P. Pedoto, Ph.D. – (Montclair & Sparta, NJ)
Phone: (973) 783-7772
Email: Drpedoto@embarq.com

Clinton H. Scott, Ph.D. – (Trenton, NJ)
South Broad St. Counseling Services
Addictive behavior, ADD/ADHD, adolescent issues, anxiety, bipolar, depression, obsessive-compulsive, rape, sexual behavior, religious issues, trauma
Phone: (609) 394-8000
Email: sbscservice@aol.com

Rachel Shemesh, MA – (Oradell, NJ)
Addictive behavior, ADD/ADHD, adolescent issues, anxiety, bipolar, depression, coping skills, eating disorders, rape, sexual behaviors, sleep disorders, trauma
Phone: (201) 739-4504
Email: rshemesh@ncfl.net

Mary Ellen Stanisci, Ph.D. – (Lincroft, NJ)
Phone: (732) 671-0196

Laurie Patlin Suttenberg, LCSW, DCSW – (Cherry Hill, NJ)
Addictive behavior, adolescent issues, anxiety, depression, coping skills, eating disorders, PTSD, social skills training, stress management
Phone: (856) 435-4793
Email: LaurieFSPS@aol.com

John Viterito, LPC – (Monmouth Junction, NJ)
Phone: (732) 438-0118
Email: jvlpc@aol.com

NEW YORK:

Henry Arroyo, DAC, LCSW, CASAC, DCSW – (Forrest Hills, NY)
H &L Counseling Services
Addictive behavior, adolescent issues, anxiety, coping skills, depression, employee assistance, PTSD, sexual behavior, stress management, violence
Phone: (718) 459-5100
Email: HLCounseling@aol.com

Rochelle Balter, Ph.D. – (New York, NY)
Phone: (917) 783-6877
Email: RBalt@aol.com

Carun Baruch-Feldman – (Scarsdale, NY)
Phone: (914) 646-9030
Email: DrCarenFeldman@msn.com

Irving Becker, Ed.D. – (Brooklyn, NY)
Phone: (718) 259-4592
Phila71@aol.com

Kerry Betensky, Ph.D. – (East Hills, NY)
Children & Adolescents
Phone: (516) 626-8353
Email: kabetensky@aol.com

James K. Bowman, Psy.D. – (Merrick & New York, NY)
Phone: (347) 685-7393
Email: Bowmanjk86@cs.com

William Boylan, LCSW, CCBT, CASAC – (New York, NY)
East Village Therapy
Addictive behavior, anxiety, obsessive-compulsive, PTSD, stress management
Phone: (917) 587-6959
Email: wboylan@nyc.rr.com

Ana Cohen, Ph.D. – (New York, NY)
Phone: (646) 265-0473
Email: Arc29@cornell.edu

Raymond DiGiuseppe, Ph.D. – (Hempstead, NY)
Phone: (516) 538-9427; (718) 990-1955 (VM)
Email: Digiuser@stjohns.edu

Rev. Thomas V. Downes, Ph.D. – (Brooklyn, NY)
Interfaith problems, weight loss, relationship problems
Phone: (718) 522-1799
Email: downestein@webtv.net

Albert Ellis Institute – (New York, NY)
Phone: (212) 535-0822
Email: info@albertellis.org
Website: www.albertellis.org
Practitioners:
F. Michler Bishop, Ph.D.: fmbishop@aol.com
Raymond DiGiuseppe, Ph.D.: digiuser@stjohns.edu
Kristene A. Doyle, Ph.D.: krisdoyle@albertellis.org
Robert Fried, Ph.D.: rfriedphd@earthlink.net
J. Ryan Fuller, Ph.D.: rfuller@albertellis.org
Wilson McDermut, Ph.D.: mcdermuw@stjohns.edu
Dana Moriarty, Ph.D.: dglieber@msn.com
Siobhan O'Leary, MA: siobhanoleary@gmail.com

Richard Pecoroni, MA: Richard@pathwaystopotential.com
Steven Schwartz, MA: shschwartzod@hotmail.com

Jo Ann Engelhardt, RN, BSN, MS – (Southhampton, NY)
Addictive behavior, anxiety, bipolar, depression, coping skills, obsessive-compulsive, psychopharmacology, social skills training, stress management
Phone: (631) 283-6849
Email: jaze@optonline.net

Mark Galloway, MSW – (Baldwin, NY)
Adolescent issues, ADD/ADHD, anxiety, depression, coping skills, employee assistance, schizophrenia, sexual behavior, social skills training
Phone: (516) 528-5876
Email: mgalloway@optonline.net

Andrea Garry, Psy.D. – (Hartsdale, NY)
Phone: (914) 328-0108
Email: drgarry@optonline.net

Ethel Geller, Ph.D. – (New York, NY)
Phone: (212) 861-7521

William L. Golden, Ph.D. – (New York & Briarcliff Manor, NY)
Phone: (212) 737-2701; (914) 762-2986
Email; williamgolden@optonline.net

Richard Grallo, Ph.D. – (New York, NY)
Metropolitan College of New York
Phone: (212) 343-1234 x2407

Patricia Hunter, Ph.D. – (New York, NY)
Phone: (212) 229-0595
Email: Phunter77.47@earthlink.net

Jamie Joseph, Ph.D. – (Hicksville & Port Jefferson Station, NY)
Depression, anger, women's issues, couple's counseling and eating disorders
Phone: (516) 933-8586; (631) 476-5984
Email: jjoseph97@hotmail.com

Peter S. Kanaris, Ph.D. – (Smithtown, NY)
Phone: (631) 979-2640
Email: DrPit1@aol.com

Steven G. Katz, Ph.D. – (Garden City & New York, NY)
Phone; (516) 747-1093; (212) 288-4546
Email: Sgk422@aol.com

Richard E. Madden, LCSW, Ph.D. – (Catskill, NY)
Adolescent issues, anxiety, bipolar, depression, hypnosis, obsessive-compulsive, pain management, PTSD, sleep disorders, social skills training
Phone: (518) 943-1000
Email: madden@thestressdoc.com
Website: www.thestressdoc.com

Jean Mone, MSW – (New York, NY)
Jean Mone, Inc.
Addictive behavior, anxiety, depression, coping skills, EMDR, PTSD, sexual behavior, social skills training
Phone: (212) 982-5158
Email: jeanmoneinc@hotmail.com
Website: www.jeanmone.com

Jennifer B. Naidich, Ph.D. – (New York, NY)
Divorce survival, anger management, bipolar disorder
Phone: (212) 888-8688
Email: jnaidich@mac.com

Nando Mark Pelusi, Ph.D. – (New York, NY)
Addictive behavior, anxiety, coping skills, eating disorders, social skills training
Phone: (212) 947-7111 x111
Email: npelusi@mac.com
Website: www.nandopelusi.com

Edward Pino, MS – (New York, NY)
Addictive behavior, ADD/ADHD, anxiety biofeedback, coping skills, depression, eating disorders, hypnosis, pain management, PTSD, stress management
Phone: (646) 734-7114
Email: edpino@mac.com

Mitchell Robin, Ph.D. – (New York, NY)
Phone: (212) 947-7111 x215
Email: askdrmitch@drmitch.org
Website: www.drmitch.org

Daniel M. Rudofossi, Psy.D., Ph.D. – (New York, NY)
Complex trauma, grief, anxiety, depression
Phone: (212) 213-3102
Email: Docp37@aol.com

Rachel Romm, Ph.D. – (New York, NY)
Phone: (917) 439-6446
Email: rachelrommgoberphd@hotmail.com

Marjorie B. Sugarman, LCSW – (Smithtown, NJ)
Addictive behavior, adolescent issues, anxiety, bipolar, depression, coping skills,
eating disorders, hypnosis, obsessive-compulsive, pain management
Phone: (631) 361-7828
Email: mbsugie@optonline.net

Mark Terjesen, Ph.D. – (Jamaica, NY)
St. John's University
Phone: (718) 990-5860
Email: terjesem@stjohns.edu

Nicole S. Urdang, MS, NCC, DHM – (Buffalo, NY)
Holistic psychotherapy
Phone: (716) 882-0848
Email: urdang@buffalo.com

Virginia Waters, Ph.D. – (New York, NY)
Phone: (212) 744-4500
Email: Vwatersphd@aol.com

Paul M. Weinhold, Ph.D. – (Great Neck, Manhattan, Amagansett & NY, NY)
Phone: (516) 466-8330; (212) 459-3767
Email: zensport@verizon.net

Anita Weintraub, MSW, Ph.D. – (Staten Island, NY)
NYC Board of Education
Adolescent issues, ADD/ADHD, anxiety, coping skills, social skills training
Phone: (718) 390-1858

Janet Wolfe, Ph.D. – (New York, NY)
Couple's therapy, anxiety, depression, women's issues
Phone: (646) 515-3130
Email: janetwolfe@aol.com

NORTH CAROLINA

John P. Anderson – (Winston-Salem, NC)
Anger management and adults
Phone: (336) 413-0143
Email: Jpa@wfu.edu

Mike Cascio, MS, MSW, DCBT – (Greenville, NC)
Greenville Psychiatric Associates
Addictive behavior, ADD/ADHD, anxiety, bipolar, depression, coping skills,
PTSD, pre-marital therapy, rape, sexual behavior, stress management, trauma

Phone: (252) 758-4810
Email: mcascio4@excite.com

Bruce Eads, LCSW - (Raleigh, NC)
Phone: (919) 412-7069
Email: beads@nc.rr.com

Laurel Link – (Winston-Salem, NC)
NC Baptist Hospital
Anxiety, coping skills, depression, pain management, phobias, PTSD, religious issues, stress management, trauma
Phone: (336) 716-0854
Email: llink@wfubmc.edu

Dr. Linda S. Patton, Ed.D. – (Clyde, NC)
The Life Counseling Center, P.A.
Addictive behavior, anxiety, eating disorders, PTSD, religious issues, schizophrenia, stress management, trauma
Phone: (828) 627-5433
Email: drlpatton@bellsouth.net

OHIO:

Kenneth G. Alexander, M.Ed. – (Cleveland, OH)
Cleveland Clinic Hospital
Addictive behavior, adolescent issues, coping issues, depression, religious issues, sexual behavior, stress management
Phone: (216) 444-8739
Email: Alexank@ccf.org
Website: www.clevelandclinic.org

Kathleen A. Barnett, LISW, CCBT, BC, ACSW – (Cincinnati, OH)
Adolescent issues, alcohol abuse, anxiety, coping skills, depression, employee assistance, PTSD, rape, religious issues, schizophrenia, social skills training
Phone: (513) 742-2816

Diane S. Bellas, LPCC-S – (Richmond Heights, OH)
Anxiety, coping skills, depression, employee assistance, PTSD, religious issues, social skills training, stress management, trauma
Phone: (216) 738-0819

Kathleen T. Burton, Ph.D. – (Lakewood, OH)
Personal Growth and Human Relations
Anxiety, depression, PTSD, pre-marital therapy, rape, social skills training, stress management, trauma
Phone: (216) 227-9481

Email: Ktburtonphd@yahoo.com

John J. Gary, MS, PCC-S, Ph.D. – (Worthington, OH)
Addictive behavior, adolescent issues, anxiety, bipolar, depression, coping skills,
eating disorders, hypnosis, PTSD, sleep disorders, stress management
Phone: (614) 846-8800
Email: JonieJoe@columbus.rr.com

John M. Heilmeier, MSW, LISW – (St. Clairsville, OH)
Adolescent issues, ADD/ADHD, anxiety, biofeedback, bipolar, depression,
coping skills, eating disorders, hypnosis, pain management, schizophrenia
Phone: (740) 695-3924
Email: johnheilmeier@gmail.com

Dr. Lee Horowitz, Ph.D. – (Beachwood, OH)
Lee J. Horowitz, Ph.D., Inc.
Addictive behavior, adolescent issues, anxiety, bipolar, coping skills, depression,
eating disorders, hypnosis, pain management, stress management
Phone: (216) 831-2700
Email: doctorleej@aol.com

Lisa Montgomery – (Columbus, OH)
Sounding Board Counseling Center
Anxiety, bipolar, depression, coping skills, obsessive-compulsive, PTSD, rape,
self-injurious behavior, social skills training, stress management
Phone: (614) 231-1164

OKLAHOMA:

Charlotte Burrough, LCSW – (Ada, OK)
Christian Counseling Plus
Adolescent issues, ADD/ADHD, anxiety, bipolar, depression, coping skills,
EMDR, PTSD, religious issues, social skills training, stress management
Phone: (580) 436-9099
Email: charlotte@wpswireless.com
Website: www.cccognitvetherapy.com

Terri Hausam, MSW – (Tulsa, OK)
Laureate Psychiatric Hospital and Clinic
Adolescent issues, alcohol abuse, anxiety, bipolar, depression, coping skills,
PTSD, parenting, sexual behavior, sleep disorders, stress management
Phone: (918) 491-3700
Email: tlhausam@saintfrancis.com

Lillian Kay Johndrow, MS – (Bartlesville, OK)
Cherokee Nation Behavior Health

Addictive behavior, adolescent issues, anxiety, bipolar, depression, coping skills, PTSD, rape, religious issues, social skills training, trauma
Phone: (918) 336-0823
Email: cherokay@aol.com

Joel S. Leitch, MS – (Tulsa, OK)
Family Medical Care
Addictive behavior, ADD/ADHD, adolescent issues, anxiety, bipolar, depression, coping skills, eating disorders, pain management, PTSD, sleep disorders, rape
Phone: (918) 493-7850
Email: jleitch@fmct.com
Website: www.fmct.com

OREGON:

Hank Robb III, Ph.D., ABPP – (Lake Oswego, OR)
Phone: (503) 635-2489
Email: robbhb@pacificu.edu

PENNSYLVANIA:

Michael S. Broder, Ph.D. – (Philadelphia, PA)
Phone: (215) 545-7000
Email: DrBroder@aol.com
Website: www.DrMichaelBroder.com

Dr. Natalie Charney, Ph.D. – (Philadelphia, PA)
Addictive behavior, anxiety, bipolar, depression, coping skills, employee assistance, obsessive-compulsive, PTSD, social skill training, trauma
Phone: (215) 725-6080
Email: ncharney@verizon.net

Cynthia Comparato, MA, MSW, LCSW – (New Hope, PA)
New Hope Center for Cognitive Therapy
Anxiety, bipolar, depression, coping skills, eating disorders, hypnosis, obsessive-compulsive, stress management
Phone: (215) 622-3717

Keith Ferrell, MA, CAC – (Wilkes-Barre, PA)
Mood disorders, anxiety disorders, addictions, marriage counseling
Phone: (570) 826-0999
Email: DKFerrel@ptd.net

Doreen John, MA – (Kingston, PA)
Adolescent issues, anxiety, coping skills, obsessive-compulsive, PTSD, social skills training, stress management

Phone: (570) 283-2040

Anne Marie Kopec, ACSW, CAC – (Kingston, PA)
Children/sexual abuse, sexually reactive behavior
Phone: (570) 430-0521
Email: amkopec@aol.com

Deane Lappin, Psy.D. – (Paoli, PA)
Anxiety, coping skills, depression, EMDR, obsessive-compulsive, parenting, sexual behavior, social skills training, stress management
Phone: (610) 644-4666
Email: deane@lappin.com

Carol Larach, MSEd, MPH – (Philadelphia, PA)
Depression
Phone: (215) 893-9156
Email: clarach@aol.com

Donna L. Lauck, DNSc, APRN, BC – (Abington, PA)
Collaborative Care of Abington
Addictive behavior, anxiety, bipolar, depression, coping skills, employee assistance, hypnosis, parenting, PTSD, stress management, trauma
Phone: (215) 884-1776
Email: cpsych99@aol.com
Website: www.collaborativecare.org

Karen Markle, - (Pittsburgh, PA)
NHS Human Services
ADD/ADHD, pre-marital therapy, social anxiety, social skills training
Phone: (412) 247-5780 x226
Email: kmarkle@nhsonline.org
Website: www.hnsonline.org

Dr. Daniel J. Pezzulo, Ph.D. – (Lancaster, PA)
Behavioral Healthcare Consultants
Addictive behaviors, ADD/ADHD, adolescent issues, anxiety, bipolar, depression, coping skills, employee assistance, parenting, PTSD
Phone: (717) 581-5255
Email: Daje42@gmail.com

Dr. Beverly Steinfeld, Ph.D. – (Pittsburgh, PA)
Anxiety, depression, coping skills, EMDR, PTSD, rape, stress management
Phone: (412) 421-8307

Mark Tulin – (Philadelphia, PA)
Adolescent issues, ADD/ADHD, anxiety, depression, eating disorders,

obsessive-compulsive, pain management, PTSD, rape, stress management
Phone: (215) 327-6663
Email: mftulin@hotmail.com

Richard Whitmire, MSW – (Danville, PA)
Addictive behavior, anxiety, depression, coping skills, employee assistance, hypnosis, PTSD, pre-marital therapy, stress management
Phone: (570) 271-1129
Email: whitmire@PTD.net

James A. Wrable, Ph.D. – (Philadelphia, PA)
Anxiety, ADD/ADHD, bipolar, depression, eating disorders, obsessive-compulsive, PTSD, social skills training, stress management
Phone: (215) 480-9430
Email: wrabs@att.net

RHODE ISLAND:

Craig M. Canover, MS, LMHC, CAGS – (West Greenwich, RI)
Addictive behavior, ADD/ADHD, adolescent issues, anxiety, depression, coping skills, obesity, obsessive-compulsive, parenting, PTSD, stress management
Phone: (401) 441-4490
Email: Conover9@cox.net

Herman Lowe, Ph.D. – (Providence, RI)
Phone: (401) 272-8860
Email: hermanlowe@comcast.net

SOUTH CAROLINA:

Carey A. Washington, Ph.D. – (Colmia, SC)
Addictive behavior, ADD/ADHD, adolescent issues, anxiety, depression, eating disorders, obsessive-compulsive, sexual behavior, stress management
Phone: (803) 699-1115
Email: caw405@msn.com

TENNESSEE:

Gerri Bishop, Ph.D. – (Cordova, TN)
Phone: (901) 388-1893
Email: gerribishopwork@comcast.net; gerribishop@comcast.net

Ed Nottingham, Ph.D., ABPP – (Memphis, TN)
Phone: (901) 580-4316
Email: nottigham@bellsouth.net

James V. Woods, M.Ed. – (Jackson, TN)
State of Tennessee (DMRS)
Addictive behavior, ADD/ADHD, adolescent issues, bipolar, depression, coping skills, obsessive-compulsive, rape, stress management
Phone: (731) 423-2186
Email: james.woods@state.tn.us

TEXAS:

Robert N. Dain, Ph.D., ABPP – (Dallas, TX)
Depression, anxiety/panic
Phone: (214) 350-7171
Email: rdain@mac.com

George Gonzalez, Ph.D. – (Harlingen, TX)
Immaculate Heart of Mary Parish
Phone: (956) 266-1813
Email: fathergonzalez@hotmail.com

Lynnette Greak, LPC – (Lubbock, TX)
Lynnette Greak, Med, LPC
Adolescent issues, anxiety, depression, coping skills, eating disorders, pain management, PTSD, religious issues, sleep disorders, stress management
Phone: (806) 794-4261
Email: Lynnettegreak-1pc@skyglobal.net

Lisa H. Lang, Ph.D. – (Flower Mound, TX)
Life Skills Unlimited
Addictive behavior, adolescent issues, anxiety, depression, coping skills, eating disorders, hypnosis, PTSD, rape, sexual behavior, sleep disorders, trauma
Phone: (972) 724-0748
Email: drlang@tx.rr.com
Website: www.lifeskillsunlimited.com

James Lathrop, LCSW, BCD – (Corpus Christi, TX)
Phone: (361) 887-9639
Email: james@24-7-help.com

Stacie McKenna-Crochet, MSW – (Austin, TX)
Addictive behavior, adolescent issues, bipolar, depression, coping skills, eating disorders, obsessive-compulsive, PTSD, rape, social skills training
Phone: (512) 921-5925
Email: info@staciecrochet.com
Website: www.staciecrochet.com

Janice M. Roberson, MS – (Mansfield, TX)
For Couples Only
Addictive behavior, bipolar, coping skills, depression, eating disorders,
obsessive-compulsive, parenting, pre-marital therapy, stress management
Phone: (817) 773-4195

Earl Salzman, Ph.D. – (Houston, TX)
Phone: (281) 493-3632

Clayton T. Shorkey, Ph.D. – (Austin, TX)
Phone: (512) 471-0520
Email: cshorkey@mail.utexas.edu

Pat Tebbs-Gates, LPC, LCDC – (San Antonio, TX)
Pat Tebbs-Gates Counseling
Addictive behavior, adolescent issues, anxiety, bipolar, depression, coping skills,
eating disorders, obsessive-compulsive, social skills training, parenting
Phone: (210) 521-9330
Website: www.texastherapists.com/PatTebbsGates.html

Dr. Ron Terry, Psy.D., LMSW – (Houston, TX)
Harris County Hospital District
Addictive behavior, adolescent issues, AIDS/HIV infection, anxiety, depression,
coping skills, obesity, PTSD, psychopharmacology, rape, schizophrenia
Phone: (713) 873-4025
Email: ron_terry@hchd.tmc.edu

UTAH:

Donna E. Castleton, DSW – (Murray, UT)
Intermountain Center for Cognitive Therapy
Addictive behavior, adolescent issues, anxiety, depression, coping skills,
obsessive-compulsive, parenting, PTSD, social skills training, trauma
Phone: (801) 268-2887

Donald E. Goff, Ph.D. – (St. George, UT)
Red Rock Canyon School
Addictive behavior, ADD/ADHD, adolescent issues, anxiety, bipolar, depression,
coping skills, eating disorders, PTSD, rape, religious issues, stress management
Phone: (435) 673-6111
Email: donaldegoff@hotmail.com

Anick Malmstrom, M.Ed – (Provo, UT)
Wasatch Mental Health
Anxiety, bipolar, depression, coping skills, obsessive-compulsive, sexual
behavior, social skills training, stress management, trauma, violence

Phone: (801) 373-9656

VERMONT:

B. Marshall Hammond, M.Ed. – (Rutland, VT)
Cornerstone Design Group
Obsessive-compulsive, pre-marital therapy, rape, sexual behavior, trauma
Phone: (888) 775-2405
Email: cornerstone@vermontel.net
Website: www.cornerstonedesignsgroup.ws

VIRGINIA:

Katherine Cabaniss, Ph.D. – (Victoria, VA)
Adolescent issues, anxiety, depression, coping skills, hypnosis, parenting, social skills training, stress management
Email: DrCabaniss@yahoo.com
Website: www.PsychEdCourses.com

Steven M. Harner, Psy.D. – (Falls Church, VA)
Adolescent issues, ADD/ADHD, anxiety, bipolar, depression, coping skills, eating disorders, self-injurious behavior, social skills training, parenting
Phone: (703) 533-3930
Email: DrSteveHarner@gmail.com
Website: www.thestonehouse.ws

Gabriele Neumaier-Farnsworth, LCSW – (Fredericksburg, VA)
ADD/ADHD, anxiety, bipolar, coping skills, depression, employee assistance, hypnosis, PTSD, self-injurious behavior, social skills training, trauma
Phone: (540) 371-3637
Email: gaby518@cs.com

Paul J. Woods, Ph.D. – (Roanoke, VA)
Phone: (540) 265-1949

WASHINGTON:

Lyn Criddle, Ph.D. – (Seattle, WA)
Phone: (206) 624-1552
Email: wilcrddl@aol.com; lcridl@gmail.com

Eric Smeltz, Psy.D., ABPP – (Spokane, WA)
Phone: (509) 981-9999

WEST VIRGINIA:

Dr. Ed Jacobs, Ph.D. – (Star City, WV)
Impact Therapy Associates
Addictive behavior, adolescent issues, anxiety, depression, eating disorders, phobias, PTSD, pre-marital therapy, social skills training
Phone: (304) 599-0109
Email: edjacobs@impacttherapy.com
Website: www.impacttherapy.com

Patti Miller, MA, LPC, NCC, CCBT, CCAC, ALPS – (Inwood, WV)
ADD/ADHD, anxiety, bipolar, depression, obsessive-compulsive, panic disorders, stress management
Phone: (304) 229-9242

Dr. Aldo R. Pucci, Psy.D., LPC – (Weirton, WV)
Rational Living Therapy Institute
Addictive behavior, ADD/ADHD, adolescent issues, anxiety, depression, coping skills, eating disorders, hypnosis, pain management, PTSD, stress management
Phone: (304) 723-3982
Email: aldo@rational-living-therapy.org
Website: www.rational-living-therapy.org

Michele Young, LICSW, BCD – (Barboursville, WV)
Phone: (304) 736-8004

WISCONSIN:

Mary E. Bonneson, MS, LPC, NCC – (Wauwatosa, WI)
Family Care Psychological Services
Adolescent issues, ADD/ADHD, anxiety, bipolar, depression, coping skills, eating disorders, employee assistance, religious issues, social skills training
Phone: (414) 771-5002
Email: MaryBCares@aol.com

Bill Borcherdt, ACSW – (Menasha & Waupaca, WI)
Phone: (920) 722-4835; (920) 722-4838
Email: bborcherdt2@new.rr.com

Henry Steinberger, Ph.D. – (Madison, WI)
Substance abuse, Smart recovery
Phone: (608) 238-5176 x352
Email: steinberger@sbcglobal.net

Brian A. Wolf, Ph.D. – (Kenosha, WI)
Professional Services Group
Addictive behavior, ADD/ADHD, adolescent issues, anxiety, bipolar, depression, coping skills, PTSD, self-injurious behavior, stress management

Phone: (262) 652-2406

WYOMING:

Kay Cartee, Psy.D. – (Riverton, WY)
Christian Counseling Center
Addictive behavior, adolescent issues, AIDS/HIV infection, anxiety, bipolar, depression, coping skills, PTSD, rape, religious issues, social skills training
Phone: (307) 690-0661
Email: daughterofgolda@yahoo.com

Steven D. Roth, MA, LPC, CCBT – (Sheridan, WY)
Normative Services, Inc.
Addictive behavior, ADD/ADHD, adolescent issues, anxiety, biofeedback, bipolar, depression, coping skills, schizophrenia, self-injurious behavior
Phone: (307) 672-5464
Email: Diogenes16@juno.com

SECTION VIII-TREATMENT PROGRAMS

PART ONE: TREATMENT CENTERS IN UNITED STATES WHO OFFER CHOICES BEYOND 12-STEP APPROACH

3HO Super Health – (Tucson, AZ)
(888) 346-2420
yogainfo@3HO.org
www.3ho.org
>   Offers inpatient program that is a well-balanced whole-person approach. Provides time proven technology and sacred science of Kundalini Yoga, meditation, a healthy, vegetarian diet and a philosophy of compassion and kindness.

A Better Way to Recover – (Palm Springs, CA)
(760) 325-1403
drheward@gmail.com
www.hellopalmsprings.com/ABetterWayToRecover.cfm
>   An outpatient program that utilizes only safe and effective, FDA-approved medications, including the anti-craving medication Naltrexone and the relapse prevention medication Campral, as well as one-on-one counseling sessions. Attendance at some non-12 step recovery support group meetings is suggested.

Accelerated Recovery – (Atlanta, GA)
(877) 786-7454
www.iwanttostopnow.com
>   Begins with private detoxification services and continues with intensive 1,2, and 3 week individualized treatment as well as outpatient programs and aftercare. Claim success rates up to 8 times the national average. Believe there is a permanent solution to problem of alcoholism and they guarantee your success. First company in nation to implement the Combined Recovery Protocol, which combines pharmacology, medical management, focused therapy and wellness management, confirmed to be the most effective type of treatment for alcohol addiction by one of the largest studies ever done by the National Institute on Alcohol Abuse and Alcoholism.

Ackerman Institute for the Family – (New York, NY)
(212) 879-4900
ackerman@ackerman.org
www.ackerman.org/centers/substanceAbuseAndTheFamily/index.html
>   Center for Substance Abuse and the Family (CSAF) brings families together in an outpatient setting to address the previously unrecognized consequences of substance abuse and to share perspectives about the impact of alcohol and drugs on their relationships and to generate new strategies for tackling the unwanted consequences of substance abuse on family life.

109

A Cup of Tea – (Asheville, NC)
(828) 254-6620
http://newfrontier.com/acupoftea/cravings.htm
    Offer weekend or 7 day retreats, using a holistic and conscious, spiritual approach to the elimination of cravings, by showing the interrelated causes of one's behavior. Use methods such as supportive counseling, breathwork, dietary supplements, guided imagery, yoga and behavioral modification.

Addiction Alternatives – (Los Angeles, CA)
(310) 275-LIFE
Habit.@aa2.org
www.addictionalternatives.com
    Provides non 12-step based medical/behavioral program, individually tailored to meet each client's needs. Clients may choose abstinence or moderation, and services include brief or intensive in-person or telephone cognitive-behavioral sessions, groups and family sessions. Brain wave testing is also offered for objective neurological assessments.

Alcohol Management Program – (nationwide)
(800) 222-5145; (734) 647-6691
http://www.med.umich.edu/mfit/alcoholmanagement/index.htm
    Brief, confidential educational program to help client eliminate drinking problems by reducing drinking or stopping completely, depending on what client chooses. The program is for people with mild to moderate alcohol problems, not for those who are severely dependent. See end of part 2 for therapists providing Alcohol Management Program training.

Alta Mira Treatment Programs – (Sausalito, CA)
(866) 922-1350
http://altamirarecovery.com
    Offers inpatient individualized treatment to recreate your path through blending both conventional and integrative services including, but not limited to a medical, psychological and nutritional assessment, individual, group and family therapy, oral and dietary nutrient therapy to rebalance brain and body chemistry quickly, regular body work such as exercise, yoga, massage and acupuncture and attendance at support group meetings of your choice.

Alternative Recovery Options at Capitol Associates, LLC – (Madison, WI)
(608) 238-5176
steinberger@sbcglobal.net
    Provides outpatient, individualized brief, or long-term guidance and treatment for addictive behaviors (alcohol, substance abuse, and activity addictions). Various alternative approaches including SMART, Rational Emotive Behavior Therapy and other therapies for emotional problems.

Alternative Treatment International – (Clearwater, FL)

(800) 897-8060
www.alternative2rehab.com
Non-12 step individualized recovery for substance abuse and dual-diagnosed. Use Perception Therapy®, relapse prevention, nutritional counseling, yoga and more. Offer residential, intensive outpatient, outpatient, and aftercare services.

Americas Addiction Treatment, Inc. – (Charlotte, NC)
(704) 806-0394
SRYoung111@aol.com
Offers full range of outpatient treatment with main interest in cognitive-behavioral, existential and humanistic approaches.

A Positive Alternative: Women's Recovery Center and Men's Recovery Program and College Student Program to Prevent Addiction – (Seattle, WA)
(206) 453-1847
www.apositivealternative.com
Offer a non-12-step outpatient program, with separate groups for men and women. Believe that recovery is based on client's sense of empowerment and choice. Use University of Washington's Pilot study of "mindfulness for the prevention of relapse" to reduce relapse and Motivational Enhancement methods are used to allow the power to choose abstinence to come from each individual's deepest values. Continue to incorporate the latest scientific research that has proven to be effective with addictive behavior.

Assisted Recovery Centers – (various locations & online program)
(800) 527-5344 (main number)
(314) 645-6840 (Phoenix, AZ); (702) 248-2061 (Las Vegas, NV)
(888) 570-6391 (Savannah, GA)
www.assistedrecovery.com
Believe that addiction is a brain-based disorder that is medically treatable, and for the first time in nearly 50 years, a medication has been approved for the treatment of alcohol and opiate dependence. Offer detox, outpatient, intensive outpatient, accelerated program, confidential executive program and alcohol harm reduction program.

Azure Acres Treatment Center – (Northern CA & online program)
(800) 222-7292
www.azureacres.com
Since 1954, they have been providing a broad range of treatment options, for adults and adolescents, for drug and alcohol abuse and gambling addiction. Detox, outpatient, and aftercare available.

Bay Recovery Centers, Inc. – (San Diego, CA)
(800) 375-7263
www.bayrecovery.com

Provides blend of medical, social and psycho-educational models of treatment to address substance abuse and pain disorders. Licensed buphrenorphine and suboxone services, dual-diagnosis system management, relapse prevention, denial therapy, nutrition education and 12-step model. Offer residential, outpatient, continuing care and family programs.

Bayside Marin – (San Rafael, CA)
(800) 757-7131
www.baysidemarin.com
Emphasize individually tailored approach, including relapse prevention, mood management, family groups. Expose clients to many self-help programs, such as 12-step, SMART, LifeRing and Women for Sobriety. Provides intervention services, detox, inpatient, outpatient and continuing care.

Bradford Recovery Systems- (Bradford, PA)
(814) 362-8319
www.brmc.com
Specialize in dual-diagnosis. Therapists meet one-on-one with clients to formulate an individualized treatment plan. May include group therapy offering information on health issues, life skills, women's issues, gambling counseling and family group sessions. Also, bi-weekly SMART Recovery support group meetings. Offer detox, inpatient and intensive outpatient.

Breakthrough Addiction Recovery – (Norcross, GA)
(770) 933-6846
www.breakthroughaddictionrecovery.com
A medically and clinically based intensive outpatient detox and treatment facility. Provide psychiatric and psychological assessments and treat co-occurring disorders such as depression, anxiety and grief. Combine individual and group therapy with cognitive behavioral therapy and FDA approved medications that help prevent cravings.

Brookside Institute – (Southern California)
(866) 405-8787
www.brooksideinstitute.com
Scientific, medical approach goes beyond traditional 12-step models while simultaneously treating emotional and behavioral disorders. Uses mainly Pennsylvania Model. They have detox, residential, outpatient, and sober living accommodations.

Casa Palmera – (Del Mar, CA)
(888) 230-5433
www.casapalmera.com
Offer a truly individualized treatment program, aiming to not just treat the symptoms, but to identify the underlying causes of the problem. Treatments range from 12-step and cognitive-behavioral to oxygen and drum therapy, and

everything in between. Residential, outpatient and extended care are available.

Celebrate Recovery – (Lake Forest, CA & nationwide)
info@celebraterecovery.com
www.celebraterecovery.com
     This is a faith-based recovery program. Purpose is to "fellowship and celebrate God's healing power in our lives through the '8 Recovery Principles'" By growing spiritually, become free from any addictive, compulsive behaviors.

Challenges – (Margate, FL)
(888) 755-3334
www.challenges-program.com
     Specializes in chronic relapse and dual diagnosis. Committed to providing individualized and goal oriented treatment. Offers residential living, outpatient and aftercare.

Changes by Choice – (Durham, NC)
(919) 416-4800
www.changesbychoice.com
     Provide comprehensive, evidence-based outpatient treatment for substance abuse, addiction and other compulsive behaviors. Approach is grounded in motivational enhancement theory. Treatment goals and components are negotiated and individually tailored. Clients can choose from a range of options, such as EMDR, acupuncture, meditation, individual, couples, family ad group counseling, including SMART Recovery, mood and anger management for men ad dialectical behavior therapy (DBT) for women. Medication-assisted treatment may be combined with counseling to facilitate detoxification, reduce craving and ease withdrawal.

Clearview – (Los Angeles, CA)
(800) 573-0770
www.clearviewtreatment.com
     Believe in individualized treatment plans, combining traditional 12-step with diet and nutrition assessment, fitness, life stress coping skills, yoga, vocational assessment, relapse prevention and more. Offer inpatient, day and evening outpatient and aftercare.

Custom Your Care at the Sea – (Laguna Beach, CA)
(800) 281-5133
www.executiverehab.com
     Believe in individualized, holistic treatment plans, combining the best in modern treatment with alternative healing. Offers intervention services, detox, inpatient and aftercare.

Decision Point Center – (Prescott, AZ)
(877) 772-3648

info@decisionpointcenter.com
www.decisionpointcenter.com
Belief that trauma is core issue of addictions so this program applies wide variety of modalities to deal with this, such as traditional and experiential therapies, adventure, ropes and equine therapies, somatic experiencing, breath work, trauma resolution as well as 12-step work.

De Paul Treatment Center – (Portland, OR)
(503) 535-1151
www.depaultreatmentcenters.org
Create fully individualized treatment plan based on strengths in key life areas and stage of recovery. Use motivational and behavioral therapy. Offer residential, intensive outpatient and continuing care for both clients and their families and separate teen program, ages 12-18.

Desert Canyon Treatment Center – (Sedona, AZ)
(888) 811-8371 x21
www.desert-canyon.com
Provides a highly personalized, comprehensive and integrated experience that focuses on building self-esteem, enhancing life-skills and helping people create a satisfying and non-addicted life. Includes repairing bio-chemical damage by drugs and alcohol, career and life program, stress reduction techniques, family program, and much more. Do not believe that addiction is a disease. Offers detox, inpatient and aftercare services.

Fairfax Hospital ARTS – (Kirkland, WA)
Addiction Recovery Treatment Services
(425) 821-2000
This treatment program is registered with SMART Recovery, and they provide evaluations (DUI, Drug Court, and voluntary). Includes relapse prevention, education program, individual counseling and Deferred Prosecution. Offers acute and sub-acute detox, intensive outpatient treatment and aftercare program.

G & G Holistic Addiction Treatment Program – (Miami, FL)
(800) 559-9503
www.holisticdrugrehab.com
Offer inpatient treatment and lifetime aftercare specializing in chronic relapsing and dual diagnosis with individualized tailored programs. Treat the whole person by using techniques such as E.M.D.R., Hypnosis, Bio-Nutritional Therapy, and Auricular acupuncture. 12-step meetings are recommended but not required.

Guided Self-Change Center at Nova South Eastern University – (Fort Lauderdale, FL)
(800) 541-6682 x5968

www.nova.edu/gsc
This program was established in 1984 in Canada by Drs. Linda and Mark Sobell. Offers outpatient services based on motivational, cognitive-behavioral modality, for people concerned about alcohol, drug, or tobacco use, gambling, weight or other life style concerns. This motivational intervention has been evaluated positively in the US, Canada, and Mexico, and emphasizes helping people take major responsibility for guiding their own change. Services in English & Spanish. Free for students and staff.

Gulf Coast Recovery – (Treasure Island, FL)
(800) 461-0641
www.gulfcoastrecovery.org
Offer wide variety of services, depending on needs and goals of individual. Combine 12-step with Bikram Yoga, good nutrition, herbs and muscle testing. Provide intervention services, residential, outpatient, sober living and aftercare.

Harm Reduction Psychotherapy and Training Associates – (New York, NY)
(877) 504-2165
info@harmreductioncounseling.com
www.harmreductioncounseling.com
Offer outpatient individualized treatment, where referrals are made for medical evaluation, outpatient detox and inpatient care when appropriate. Utilize individual psychotherapy and family and couple counseling and sees both abstinence and moderation management as acceptable goals. This results in an approach that tailors the treatment to fit the individual, rather than trying to make the individual fit into a treatment model.

Harm Reduction Psychotherapy Institute – (Washington, D.C.)
(202) 669-4413
results@hrpi.org
www.hrpi.org
Specializes in co-occurring disorders, such as depression, anxiety and trauma. Use modalities such as EMDR, REBT as well as DBT to produce solution focused and results oriented change, while moving at the pace you are ready to move in tackling your addiction, while both moderation or abstinence are acceptable goals.

Health Recovery Center, Inc. – (Mount Pleasant, SC & Minneapolis, MN)
(888) 988-6889 or (612) 827-7800
hrc@healthrecovery.com
www.healthrecoverycenters.com
"HRC has pioneered a powerful addition of biochemical repair and restoration." This is done by medical appointments, lab tests and nutritional counseling, and is combined with Rational Emotive Therapy. Claim 74% success rate for grads at 1-3.5 years. Offer intensive, 6-week outpatient program, or can

get *Seven Weeks to Sobriety* by Joan Mattews-Larson for self-treatment program.

Health Psychology Associates, S.C. – (Milwaukee, WI)
(414) 962-4048
http://www.hpaconnect.com/index.html
   Outpatient mental health clinic specializing not only in alcohol, drug and other addictions, but also with depression, anxiety and stress, obsessive/compulsive disorder, transitional life experiences, grief and loss issues and biofeedback. Provides individual, marital, family and group counseling.

Hemet Valley Recovery Center – (Hemet Valley, CA)
(800) 493-0930
www.hvrc.com
   Provide individualized treatment and patients participate in the development of their plan. Utilize 12-step, cognitive therapy, relapse prevention, educational presentations and program for the family. Also have a separate program for older adults. Offer detox, inpatient, residential, outpatient day hospital and partial day programs.

InnerBalance Health Center – (Loveland, CO)
(877) 900-7848
support@innerbalancehealthcenter.com
www.innerbalancehealthcenter.com
   Inpatient treatment that incorporates biochemical repair, talk therapy, personalized nutritional counseling and emotional and lifestyle counseling. Believe certain biochemical imbalances can make a person more prone to the addictive cycle so by restoring the chemical balance, become much more capable of overcoming addiction. Check and repair underlying physiological imbalances such as amino acid imbalance, hypoglycemia, adrenal fatigue, neurotransmitter imbalance, toxicities, nutrient deficiencies and more.

Island Grove Treatment Center- (Greeley, CO)
(970) 356-6664 ext 1179
dbrothers@gateway.net
   Believe chemical dependency is a bio-psycho-social illness, and therefore, treat the "whole" client. Registered with SMART, but also offer 12-step approach and relapse prevention. Offer detox, residential and intensive outpatient.

Journeys – (Omaha, NE)
(402) 898-4135
Elissaw@ccomaha.org
   Program specifically for adolescents. Follow a cognitive model of treatment and has individualized treatment planning for both youth and families. Offers residential, intensive outpatient treatment and aftercare.

La Frontera Center, Inc. – (Tucson, AZ)
(520) 741-2351 x221
www.lafrontera.org/admire
 An integrated, intensive program for people who are dual-diagnosed. Provide a multifaceted, client-centered approach.

Life Matters – (Singer Island, FL)
(866) 858-9478
www.lifematters.biz
 Explores the 12-steps using The Recovery Bible and integrates Bible based learning with the steps. Offer an intensive partial hospitalization/ outpatient program.

Malibu Horizon – (Malibu, CA)
(877) 338-6964
www.malibuhorizon.com
 Drug addiction is treated as a brain disease, so successful treatment methods seek to change brain chemistry or correct its imbalance, which perpetuates drug use and relapse. Detox and Dual Diagnosis specialists. Provides inpatient and aftercare.

Manchester Harmony- (Bedford, NH)
(603) 668-5200
www.harmonyfirst.com/harmonymanchester
 A medically run, outpatient program. Use the latest available medical techniques to deal with symptoms of withdrawal. Provide group therapy, introduction to various self-help groups, stress and anger management, relapse prevention tools and family groups. Offer detox and intensive outpatient program, either in morning or afternoon.

Midwest Rapid Opiate Detoxification Specialists – (Dallas, TX & Chicago, IL)
(888) 707-4673
info@mrods.com
www.mrods.com
 Provide a safe and effective method of anesthesia assisted rapid detoxification from opiates and a sound, continuing care recovery program. Also offer the Naltrexone implant as a way to ensure relapse prevention post detox.

Motivational Recovery- (Hermosa Beach, CA)
(310) 717-3138
 Individual chooses own recovery program and goal, from moderation to abstinence, and motivational recovery trained licensed therapists work with client in private, one-on-one sessions to achieve that goal. Provide Alcohol Management Program program, relapse prevention, stress management, relationship counseling, hypnosis or traditional 12 step, if that is what client

wants. Offer intensive outpatient.

Mountainside Treatment Center – (Canaan, CT)
(800) 762-5433
www.mountainside.org
Upon intake, each resident is assessed to create individualized treatment, including motivational, community based, adventure, and 12-step modalities. Offers inpatient and optional sober living environment after treatment.

Muscala Chemical Health Clinic- (Edina, MN)
(952) 920-1351
http://therapistunlimited.com/rehabs/US/MN/Minneapolis/Muscala+Chemical+Health+Clinic
Specialize in dual diagnosis and registered with SMART (you have to call for more info). Offer inpatient and partial hospitalization/day treatment.

My Way Out- (Anchorage, AK)
(206) 219-9190
www.mywayout.org
New, integrative therapy blending medication, self-administered hypnotherapy, nutritional supplements and a light exercise program. Targeted medications and herbs, including Topamax, Naltrexone and kudzu blunt neurotransmitter activity in the brain to reduce craving for alcohol. Hypnotherapy promotes positive behavioral changes in behavior. Easily administered by primary care doctor. Offers support online at discussion board. Also offers many supplements online directly from website.

NABU Medical Services – (New York, NY)
(212) 410-6832
info@nabumed.com
www.nabumed.com
Personalized outpatient detox program by Joel Nathan, MD. Detox from all substances of abuse quickly and without withdrawal symptoms. Referral available to expert addiction psychiatrists, social workers, acupuncturists and yoga instructors as needed. Utilizes Naltraxeone which decreases opiate craving. 12 step involvement is encouraged but not required.

Narcanon Freedom Treatment Program – (Albion, MI)
(800) 420-3147
www.narcononstonehawk.com
"Recognized throughout the country as the leader in residential treatment of alcohol and drug addiction." Clients learn new life skills; alcoholism is not viewed as an illness or disease. Offers **non-medical** detox, inpatient (usually 4 to 6 months).

New Dawn – (Orangevale, CA)
(866) 969-4300
info@newdawnrecovery.com
www.newdawnrecovery.com
Offers complete continuum of care, from medically monitored detox and residential treatment to day treatment, intensive outpatient and ultimately lifetime aftercare. Programs are client centered and use cognitive behavioral approach, as well as acupuncture, massage, equine therapy and dual diagnosis treatment. 12 steps are introduced and encouraged as is the right to choose alternative support groups.

New Era Health Center, Inc. – (Miami, FL)
(305) 559-8838
www.newerahealthcenter.com
Offers Sinclair Method and Pennsylvania Model, from intensive partial hospitalization to monthly medication management.

New Leaf Treatment Center – (Lafayette, CA)
(925) 284-5200
www.nltc.com
An individualized, medical approach and behavioral therapy in treatment of addictive disease and pain management. Intensive 12-week outpatient program for adolescents and adults.

North Central Health Care- (Wausau, Antigo and Merrill, WI)
(715) 848-4540; (715) 623-2394; and (715) 536-9482 respectively
www.norcen.org
Offer individualized treatment plan to meet client's needs. Provide information, education and therapy to help clients learn to make positive changes in everyday life. Groups offer opportunities to improve communication, handle stress and prevent relapse. Provide detox, inpatient and day treatment.

Our Hope – (Grand Rapids, MI) (Women only)
(616) 451-2039
www.ourhopeassociation.org
Develop individualized treatment plans based on bio-psycho-social-spiritual assessment. Combine 12-step with relaxation techniques, nutrition and assertiveness training. Offer residential and intensive outpatient.

Palm Partners – (Delray Beach, FL)
www.palmpartners.com
(877) 711-4673
Offers a holistic approach, combining 12-step model integrated with a variety of innovative and state of the art treatment strategies, including individual, group and family therapy, clinical hypnotherapy, EMDR, meditation, yoga, fitness

therapy, nutrition, life skills training, job skills training, relaxation training and rapid trauma resolution. Provides residential treatment, intensive outpatient program with or without residence, aftercare, dual diagnosis program, women's program and stress and trauma program.

Passages Treatment Center – (Malibu, CA)
(866) 761-8549
www.passagesmalibu.com
 Inpatient treatment is based upon one-on-one counseling rather than group counseling to discover and heal the underlying causes of a person's addiction. Do not believe addiction is a disease but rather a symptom caused by underlying problems. Uses holistic recovery program, including traditional Chinese medicine, (herbs and acupuncture), clinical psychology, marriage and family therapy, hypnotherapy, personal fitness, nutrition, visualization and meditation, massage and spiritual therapy.

Passages to Recovery – (Loa, UT)
(866) 625-8809
www.wildernessrecovery.com
 Wilderness, holistic treatment program incorporating conventional 12-steps and therapy with experiential journey, including backpacking, sweat lodges and a vision quest. Offer inpatient, sober living and aftercare.

Pat Moore Foundation – (Southern CA)
(800) 864-2027
www.patmoorefoundation.com
 Offers low cost treatment for people with limited or no insurance coverage. Treatment plan is individualized, including 12-step, cognitive-behavioral and motivational modalities. Also offer Christian focus program. Have detox, inpatient and outpatient programs.

Path to Recovery – (Vallejo/San Francisco Bay Area, CA)
(707) 642-6701
www.pathtorecovery.org
 Offer detox and rehab services to males over 18 years old. Recognize there are a variety of paths for each individual. Have a scientific focus and utilize the latest research about substance abuse recovery.

Pavillon International – (Mill Spring, NC)
(800) 392-4808
info@pavillon.org
www.pavillon.org
 Individualized treatment plans based on bio-psycho-social assessment. Combines traditional 12-step with educational presentations, physical wellness, equine therapy and experientially based psychotherapy. Offer intervention services and residential.

PharmaTox – (Fairfield, CA)
(707) 435-8042
www.pharmatox.com
　　　Inpatient, outpatient and transitional living facilities in San Joaquin and Solano County, using client-centered cognitive-behavioral and motivational interviewing approaches.

Practical Recovery Services – (San Diego, CA)
(858) 453-4777
www.practicalrecovery.com
　　　Offers customized, non 12-step treatment for any type of addictive behavior. It views addictive behavior as a bad habit, not as a disease. Both moderation and abstinence are supported goals. Though based in La Jolla, CA, it provides long-distance counseling services by email or phone.

Prive-Swiss (Newport Beach, CA)
(800) 866-2948; (323) 697-7278
hkunzli@betteryourbest.com
www.priveswiss.com/index.html
　　　"Exclusive, specialized intensive personal one-on-one retreat program for executives, professionals, entertainers, athletes and other high functioning, successful individual struggling with substance abuse, addictions, compulsive behaviors, burnout, stress & other issues." Provide intervention, inpatient and aftercare services.

Psychological A.R.T.S. – (Austin, TX)
(512) 343-8307
http://psycharts.com/drug-abuse.htm
　　　Provides outpatient counseling (individual, couples, family, group and hypnosis). Presents a model of substance use disorders and its treatment that is based on recent advances in cognitive science.

Reason for Recovery – (Raleigh, NC)
(919) 274-8001
www.reasonforrecovery.com
　　　Follow a learned behavior model of substance abuse and features REBT, Motivational Enhancement and SMART Meetings are available. Do not believe in disease concept of addiction. However, clients may be encouraged to attend 12-step meetings if could be helpful or if has been helpful in the past. Offer structured outpatient treatment program.

Recovery Resource Center – (Cincinnati, OH)
(513) 761-7353
www.rrci.net
　　　Work to promote choice in recovery from alcoholism, drug abuse and

other forms of addictive behaviors by holding variety of meetings, such as Women for Sobriety, SMART and LifeRing. Offer outpatient, client-centered program.

Renaissance Malibu™ – (Malibu, CA)
(888) 619-8500
www.maliburecovery.com
Believes in holistic treatment, "utilize many kinds of therapeutic approaches ranging from traditional psychological and 12-step models to alternative methods long proven to assist people in their quest for greater health, happiness and abundance." Offer inpatient program.

Responsible Recovery – (San Francisco, CA)
(510) 919-9678
www.responsiblerecovery.org
"Responsible Recovery is a sane and sensible process of discovery for individuals seeking to improve their health and change health behaviors." Developed by Dee-Dee Stout, trained in motivational interviewing, solution-focus, creative inquiry, CBT, harm reduction and more, this innovative process based on concept that individuals have their own inner strengths and solutions and are able to design goals for their lives. RR seeks to assist individuals in finding that inner wisdom and strength and to make their own decisions about the goals in their lives. Offer outpatient program.

Rutgers – The State University of NJ; Program for Addictions Consultation & Treatment (PACT)– (Piscataway, NJ)
(732) 445-6111 ext 4
www.alcoholstudies.rutgers.edu/clinical/clinprograms.html
Provides individualized outpatient services to adults and adolescents. Believe that each client is unique so treatment is planned according to needs of each individual and clients have an active role in planning of their treatment. Utilize approaches backed up by good research such as cognitive-behavioral techniques. Both SMART and 12-step meetings are available.

Schick Shadel Hospital – (Seattle, WA)
(800) 272-8464)
www.schickshadel.com
Has provided alternative treatment since 1935 using aversion therapy. This treatment "helps patients maintain healthy, productive lifestyles, free of the craving for alcohol or drugs. Give us 10 days and we'll give you back your life!"

Sierra Tuscon – (Sonoran Desert, AZ)
(800) 842-4487
www.sierratuscon.com
Use Sierra Model®, which integrates practices from medical, psychological, therapeutic and self-help communities and family systems theory.

Individualized treatment program, which may include relapse prevention, 12-step meetings, Equine Therapy, EMDR, acupuncture, cognitive-behavioral therapy and dual-diagnosis specialty groups. Offer inpatient and alumni networking resources.

Solutions For Recovery – (Dana Point, CA)
(800) 784-4791
www.solutions4recovery.com
Don't believe in "one size fits all" attitude or approach to recovery. Offer individualized treatment for inpatient, intensive outpatient and sober living environment.

Spencer Recovery Center, Inc® – (Laguna Beach, CA)
(800) 334-0394
www.spencerrecovery.com
Offer holistic approach and treatment plans are tailored to the individual. Use therapy, relapse prevention, exercise, meditation and good nutrition. Offer intervention services, inpatient, sober living, continuing care and intensive outpatient teen program.

Starlite Recovery Center – (San Antonio, TX)
(800) 292-0148
www.starliterecovery.com
Provides broad range of substance abuse treatments to adults and adolescents who suffer from alcohol and drug abuse. Offer residential, continuing care and online drug and alcohol treatment services.

St. Gregory Retreat Center – (Iowa)
(888) 778-5833
www.thesoberchoice.com/index.php
The first nationwide program, based on Dr. Stanton Peele's Life Process Program, based on skills, values, self-motivation and life-long learning. This two month in-patient program includes dietary, exercise, meditational-spiritual components as well as the most advanced cognitive-behavioral training in the addiction field. Does not believe addiction is a disease but rather a dependency brought on by one's choices and since they are choices, you control them. Program shows you how to touch base with your values and inventory your resources and assets-the positive things you come with. Living life free from substance abuse, truly accomplishing rehabilitation, is achieved through behavior modification, life-skills exercises and cognitive behavior training.

St. Joseph's Rehabilitation Center, Inc. – (Saranac Lake, NY)
(518) 891-3950
www.newyorkrehabilitation.com
Provides intervention, inpatient, outpatient and residential treatment to impoverished men and women. Offer individualized treatment plan based on

complete biopsychosocial evaluation.

St. Jude Retreat House – (Hagaman, NY)
(888) 424-2626
www.soberforever.net
A residential social/educational model of alcohol & drug addiction recovery that emphasizes the process of learning through doing, experiencing and providing positive role models. Jude Thaddeus Program has 85% permanent success rate. "Alcoholism is not a disease."

Summit Centers – (Malibu, CA)
(888) 777-9672
www.summitcenters.net
Combine 12-step program with scientifically proven treatment methods, such as cognitive-behavioral therapy, relapse prevention, mindfulness-based stress reduction, and more. Residential and aftercare provided.

Support Systems Homes, Inc. – (Northern CA)
(800) 811-1800
www.recoverythroughsupport.com
Offers individualized programs to fit client's needs. AA is mandatory. Offer group and individual therapy, communication skills, anger management. Detox, inpatient, outpatient and sober living services.

TAG, The Alexander Group – (Plane, TX)
(866) 399-2422
info@tagthealexandergroup.com
www.tagthealexandergroup.com
A intense five day program is an alternative self-help, self-improvement and empowerment program for those individuals wanting to improve their quality of life. Claim 71% of workshop attendees have restored meaning and purpose to their life and learned how to change their bad habits and poor choices.

The Center for Motivation and Change – (New York, NY)
(212) 683-3339
info@motivationandchange.com
http://motivationandchange.com
Provides outpatient individually tailored treatment plan and deals with other problems as well, such as anxiety and depression. Utilize evidence based approaches to help individuals clear difficult obstacles to gain effective, life-enhancing, long-lasting change. In addition to CMC individual and group services, provide clients at all stages of treatment with referral options for psychiatric/medication consultation as well as inpatient treatment services.

The Harm Reduction Therapy Center – (San Francisco, CA)

(415) 863-4282
info@harmreductiontherapy.org
www.harmreductiontherapy.org
     Believe that addiction is not a disease. Outpatient treatment is tailored to
the individual, taking into account each person's biological, psychological,
emotional and social issues. There is no demand for abstinence as a condition
of, or necessarily as a goal of treatment. Help person evaluate his or her
problems and plan for the right solution for themselves. Offer individual
psychotherapy, couples and family counseling, group therapy and psychiatric
medication evaluation and treatment.

The Jude Thaddeus Home Recovery Program – (Nationwide)
(888) 424-2626
info@homerecovery.net
www.homerecovery.net
     Offers a social/educational model of alcoholism and drug addiction
recovery. Alcoholism is not a disease. Can do this program at home or at St.
Jude Retreat House in New York.

The Meadows – (Wickenburg, AZ)
(800) 632-3697
www.themeadows.org
     Multi-disorder facility specializing in treatment of trauma and addiction.
Use combination of behavior modification, cognitive therapy, acupuncture, yoga
and 12-step program. Offer detox, partial hospitalization and aftercare.

The Ranch – (Nunnelly, TN)
(800) 849-5969
www.recoveryranch.com
     Believe in holistic approach, combining 12-step with ancient Toltec
wisdom, which means "to support each person in embodying love in every
decision, every thought, every action, every moment." Offer inpatient program.

The Refuge – (Ocklawaha, FL)
(866) 4REFUGE
www.therefuge-ahealingplace.com
     Inpatient program that specializes in trauma, such as PTSD as well as
substance abuse. Offer individual and group therapy, equine therapy,
hypnotherapy, breath work, yoga, psychodrama and the ropes course. 12 step
meetings are required.

The River Source – (Mesa, AZ)
(888) 687-7332
info@theriversource.org
www.theriversource.org
     Program provides inpatient care which integrates holistic, naturopathic

care with the traditional twelve step philosophy, such as yoga, meditation, IV vitamin therapy, nutritional therapy and acupuncture.

The Sand Island Treatment Center- (Honolulu, Hawaii)
The Kline-Welsh Behavioral Health Foundation
(808) 841-2319
www.sandisland.com
Individualized treatment planning, which may include cognitive-behavioral therapy, anger control group, dual-diagnosis, women's group, parenting or criminal justice group, family services, to name a few. Also provide pre-employment and transitional counseling, job search assistance, re-socialization activities and relapse prevention. Offer residential, partial hospitalization, day treatment, outpatient, sober living, after-care, follow-up services and alumni refreshing services.

The Sundance Center – (Scottsdale, AZ)
(800) 658-4880; (480) 773-7329
www.thesundancecenter.com
Believe that for programs to be successful, must be tailored to meet specific problems and concerns of the individual client. Offers inpatient, outpatient, transitional living, internet counseling and 2 years of free aftercare.

Timberline Knolls – (Chicago, IL)
(877) 257-9611
info@timberlineknolls.com
www.timberlineknolls.com
Individualized programs for women 12 and over, specializing in drug and alcohol abuse, eating disorders, co-occurring disorders, including depression, panic and anxiety, self-harming behaviors and post-traumatic stress. Offers cutting edge, evidence-based psychiatric and psychological therapeutic approaches, such as cognitive behavioral therapy, dialectical behavioral therapy, motivational interviewing, family therapy as well as encouragement in 12-step program participation. Also partner with Meier Clinics to provide Christian-based therapy for those who request this to help work through emotional and spiritual obstacles.

TLC – The Living Center – (Shoreline, WA)
(800) 719-6604
www.tlctx.com
Use TMS®, Transition, Motivation and Stabilization, a type of education and therapy, relapse prevention, plus encouragement to attend either 12-step group or other sober support group. Offer intensive outpatient.

THE THOUGHT EXCHANGE® Center for Personal Achievement-
(Morristown, NJ)
(973) 984-8244

tte@thethoughtexchange.biz
www.thethoughtexchange.biz
 Encourage personal responsibility through self-reliance. Provide information and techniques to assist clients in changing their thinking, through this thought exchange method, to create a happier and healthier life.

The Women's Health Project – (New York, NY)
(212) 523-3061
idisla@chpnet.org
www.whpnyc.org
 Provides supportive outpatient treatment environment including a range of counseling services and therapies with a focus on women who have also experienced trauma or abuse. Specializes in treatment that is designed to address issues involved in recovering from substance use in context of significant anxiety, mood and other psychiatric symptoms.

Total Health Recovery Program – (Santa Fe, NM)
(505) 310-1340
www.totalhealthrecoveryprogram.com
 Holistic individualized inpatient program using master healers and innovative diagnostic and treatment technology including acupuncture, massage, yoga, meditation, herbs, vitamins, nutritional assessment and correction, live cell blood analysis, medication review, exercise and the sweat lodge. What is offered to you is totally based on your response to each service so your day is structured by what you actually need.

Treatment Research Center at U. of Pennsylvania – (Philadelphia, PA)
(215) 222-3200 x126
 Pennsylvania model. Pharmacological and bio-psycho-social treatment, non 12-step.

Twin Town Treatment Centers – (various locations, CA)
Los Alamitos (562) 594-8844; Torrance: (310) 787-1335
North Hollywood: (818) 985-0560; Orange: (714) 532-9295
www.twintowntreatmenntcenters.com
 Outpatient programs emphasize abstinence, relapse prevention, disease model education, problem solving skills, stress management and family counseling.
Walden House – (various locations in CA)
(415) 554-1100
editor@waldenhouse.org
www.waldenhouse.com
 Behavioral health and substance abuse services based on the therapeutic community (TC) model of treatment. Depending upon individual treatment plans, clients may take part in individual and group therapy, medication services and skills training, including Dialectical Behavior Therapy skills training in

mindfulness, emotional regulation, distress tolerance and interpersonal effectiveness.

WestBridge – (Manchester, NH & Cambridge, MA)
(603) 634-4446
www.westbridge.org
Specializes in treatment of dual diagnosis, including depression, anxiety, post traumatic stress disorder and other thought or mood disorders with co-occurring substance use disorders. Utilize treatment approaches that have been researched and proven to work, such as motivational interviewing, cognitive behavioral therapy, contingency management, medication management, illness management and recovery and self help.

Weyland Consultation Services – (Walnut Creek, CA)
(925) 945-7816 x41
www.weylandservices.com
Offers individualized chemical dependency treatment programs, matching the approach to the patient's values and beliefs. Offers detox acupuncture, intensive or brief outpatient programs, and adolescent program.

Your Empowering Solutions (Y.E.S.) – (Los Angeles, CA)
(888) 541-6350
www.non12step.com
This 5 day outpatient program offers an alternative to 12-step program. Use state-of-the-art counseling treatment protocols combined with effective, anti-craving medication. Use cognitive behavioral therapy that is specifically designed to bring about behavioral change, with both moderation or abstinence being an acceptable outcome.

PART TWO: TREATMENT CENTERS OUTSIDE U.S. WHO OFFER CHOICES BEYOND 12-STEP APPROACH

A Home Away – (British Columbia, Canada)
(866) 337-3324
www.ahomeaway.org
    Offer full complement of programs, individually tailored to clients needs, including individual and couples counseling, stress management, recreation, 12-step and aftercare workshops.

Alcohol & Drug Treatment Centre – (St. Catharines, Ontario Canada)
(905) 685-5425
www.adtcniagara.ca/index.htm
    Use LifeSkills® model as a reference, where individuals are assisted in identifying areas of their life that are problematic, and in formulating goals to resolve those issues. Offer intensive outpatient, dual diagnosis program, aftercare and a relapse prevention program, which is an individual counseling option.

Behavioural Health Foundation, Inc. – (Manitoba, Canada)
(204) 269-3430
www.bhf.ca
    Offer holistic approach that deals with the contributing factors which lead to addictive behaviors. "We do not incorporate 12-step programming as it contradicts our belief that addiction is caused by many factors and is not an illness or disease." Provide long term residential treatment for men, women, dependent children and adolescent programs.

Broadreach House – (Plymouth Devon, United Kingdom)
www.broadreach-house.org.uk
    "If you choose to come to Longreach, you will participate in developing your own individually tailored treatment plan, taking into account specific underlying issues." All of their treatment methods are evidence based, such as motivational therapy, relapse prevention and support for developing practical skills for independent living. Offer detox, residential and aftercare.

Center for Addiction and Mental Health – (Toronto, Canada)
(800) 463-6273 or (416) 535-8501
www.camh.net/index.html
    Largest mental health and addiction organization in Canada and is fully affiliated with the University of Toronto. Client-centered approach recognizes everyone is different and each person has individual social, physical, emotional, spiritual and psychological needs. Care provided incorporates the preferences, needs, aspirations and cultural beliefs of individual into each treatment plan.

Channah Thailand – (Thailand)

(888)457-3518
www.channahthailand.com
channahthailand@gmail.com
"Set in a lush tropical paradise on the banks of the River Kwai, Channah offers you a Cognitive Behavioral Therapy (CBT) programme unlike anything available elsewhere in the world, and tailored to your needs."CBT will help change how you think (Cognitive) and change what you do (Behavioral).It will focus on the here and now in order to help you make the changes you want; NOW. You will also have individual and group fitness sessions, including massage and Body Renew, which is a holistic fitness system that combines movement and breathwork, which helps develop inner calm along with core body strength. Offers detox, 28-day inpatient program and aftercare services.

Clear Haven Center – (Chertsey, QC Canada; close to Montreal)
(877) 465-8080
www.clearhavencenter.com
Respect the rights of each person to make choices, especially giving them input into their own recovery program. "Using a multi-disciplinary approach and community-oriented support model based on current, well-tested and scientifically sound techniques and professional experience, these individualized programs address each client's physical, emotional, social and spiritual needs." Offer residential and aftercare

Heritage Home Foundation – (Quebec, Canada)
(866) 330-9818
Design personalized plans for each person using traditional approaches, such as cognitive-behavioral, and non-traditional, such as native healing and meditation.

Island Drug & Alcohol Service (IDAS) – (Newport, Isle of Wight England)
044 1983 526654
Email: Sue.sheer@iow.nhs.uk
Program supports both abstinence and harm reduction approaches and primarily uses cognitive-behavioral method. Offer medical detox, including methadone and buprenorphine. SMART meetings available, along with an acupuncture clinic. Outpatient services funded by National Health Service so no cost to client.

New Port Centre – (Port Colborne, Ontario Canada)
(905) 834-4501 ext. 2524
www.newportcentre.on.ca
Encourage clients to empower themselves and be more autonomous, courageous and responsible and so they allow individual to choose treatment plan that is best. Have general recovery skills tract which focuses on how thought influence feelings and behavior, 12-step tract and women's tract. Offer

short-term residential, outpatient and have recovery enhancement week twice a year for people who have had previous treatment experience.

New River Cove – (Belize, Central America)
(866) 850-2683
www.newrivercove.com
Individualized treatment plans developed to help each resident achieve mental, emotional and physical harmony. Blends traditional 12-step with progressive treatments, such as nutritional counseling, equine therapy and relapse prevention. Offers inpatient, extended care and comprehensive aftercare services.

Peace Arch Community Services – (British Columbia, Canada)
(604) 531-6226
www.pacsbc.com
Program supports both abstinence and harm reduction approaches and primarily uses cognitive-behavioral approach. Offer outpatient services, such as individual therapy and relapse prevention, funded by government, so no cost to client.

Sefton Park – (Somerset)
Phone: 01934 626371
www.sefton-park.com
Integrative approach based on individual's needs. Use various therapies, including person centered, cognitive-behavioral, solution focused and directive therapy as well as introduction to 12-step. Offer inpatient and aftercare.

The Buttery Incorporated – (Binna Burra, Australia near Byron Bay on NSW North Coast of Australia)
(02) 66872399
 www.buttery.org.au/index.php
Believe that progress in recovery from addiction is a function of development of healthy adaptive means for handling feelings. Utilizes a cognitive-behavioral approach, living skills instruction, stress management training as well as orientation to 12-step philosophy. 12-step meetings are voluntary. Offer detox, residential therapeutic community, an outreach treatment service and an outreach gambling problem service.

The Sanctuary Byron Bay – (Byron Bay, Australia)
Phone: 61-2-6685-7555
www.sanctuarybb.com
Specialize in dual-diagnosis. Believe in individualized treatments, which may include naturopathic consultation, yoga, meditation, acupuncture, therapy. 12-step participation is optional. Offer detox, residential, extended care and aftercare.

The Victoria Program – (Malaga, Spain)
+34 605-686539
http://www.addictionresourceguide.com/listings/victoria.html
   Offers a ten day intensive therapeutic treatment, and is non-12 step.

William Hitt Center- (Tijuana, Mexico)
(888) 671-9849; (888) 269-7303
http://www.williamhittcenter.com/
   Uses neurotransmitter restoration (NTR), which consists of an
intravenous solution of particular amino acids, to rebuild the damaged areas of
the brain. „The brain can then function again much more normally, cravings
disappear, stress levels become much more normal, and clarity of mind is
restored.‰ Claims to have a success rate of over 80% for long-term abstinence.
Typical NTR treatment is 10 days.

APPENDIX

Website Resources:

Please note: I have listed these resources in order to help you get further information regarding treatment and websites regarding various topics on alternatives to 12-step programs. I am not affiliated, nor do I endorse any of them… they are for informational purposes only.

www.addictionalternatives.com
　　　Provides large amount of information, including "tool box for change," links to AA alternatives and to Dr. Kern's free 15 minute consultation (See www.habitdoc.com).

Addiction Intervention Resources
www.intervene.com
　　　National addiction consulting organization that can provide intervention services, escort services to and from treatment facilities and individual mentoring.

Addiction Resource Center Inc.
www.arcinc.org
　　　Provides links to many different alternatives, and puts them into categories, according to their belief models, such as whether or not they believe it's a disease or not, spiritual, or not, etc…

Addiction Resource Guide
www.addictionresourceguide.com
　　　Can help you find treatment facility that best suits your needs.

Alcoholism: The Cause & The Cure
www.aaaacheers.com
　　　Book on how to cure the bio-chemical root cause of alcohol addiction. "Bring the holistic detox center to you!"

American Council on Alcoholism
(800) 527-5344
http://www.aca-usa.org
　　　Provides information on alcohol and drug use, treatment information, and links to various articles and websites.

www.doctordeluca.com
　　　Has many links to various articles.

Christians in Recovery
www.christians-in-recovery.com
>Provides a lot of information and resources designed to help you overcome self defeating behaviors, thoughts and addictions that you desire to change. This is a group of recovering Christians who provide mutual sharing of faith, strength and hope.

Drug and Alcohol Recovery Network (DARN)
www.darnweb.com
>Has searchable national database, including variety of treatment types.

www.habitdoc.com
>Provides free 15 minute consultation with Dr. Marc Kern, licensed clinical psychologist with over 30 years of experience or Dr. Stanton Peele, a trained addictions expert *and* attorney. Also has F.A.Q. and numerous links to other sites.

www.habitdoc/Search.cfm
>The Addiction Treatment Alternatives Provider Database provides detailed information to help you live an addiction-free, healthier life. You can find individual therapists, clinics and other professionals providing both 12-step and non-12-step therapy, plus a wide range of science-based alternative approaches and complementary medical support services.

HAMS- (Harm Reduction, Abstinence and Moderation Support)
(347) 678-5671
Hams@hamshrn.org
http://hamsnetwork.org
>Primarily provide support for people who wish to reduce or eliminate the harm in their lives caused by the use of "soft" drugs alcohol, marijuana, nicotine and/or caffeine. However, HAMS is open to all people who wish to reduce or eliminate the harm in their lives caused by any substance or any behavior.

Joint Commission on the Accreditation of Healthcare Organizations-
(Oakbrook Terrace, IL)
www.jcaho.org
>Website includes searchable quality-check database, so you can put in name of center, and its status and info will be located. (Facilities for alcoholism/addiction are under category "behavioral health.")

National Alliance of Methadone Advocates- (New York, NY)
(212) 595-NAMA
www.methadone.org
>Website includes lists of methadone providers, links to websites; good place to start for methadone information.

Nine Step Pagans
http://ninesteppagans.faithweb.com
Initiated as Pagan-friendly, but not other-exclusive, alternative to Judaeo-Christian oriented recovery groups, internet e-group support group, with online chat meetings.

The Drug and Alcohol Prevention Network
www.drugnet.net
Has links to many other pages for treatment, self-help groups, etc.

The Orange Papers
www.orange-papers.org/orange-effectiveness.html
Numerous essays written by an ex-AA member portraying, in great detail, the "lies" of AA, including *Religious Roots of the 12 Steps, The 12 Biggest Secrets of AA, The Funny Spirituality of Bill Wilson and AA* and much, much more.

Positive Atheism Magazine
www.positeatheism.org
A huge amount of articles, mainly regarding the trends of courts finding it unconstitutional to mandate sentencing to 12-step programs, deeming them "undeniably religious."

Stanton Peele Site
www.peele.net/lib/index.html
Extensive collection of articles written by Stanton Peele.

Penn & Teller's show "Bull ***" on Showtime
www.sho.com/site/ptbs/topics.do?topic=12
Penn & Teller devoted this show to what they called "12-step Lies."

www.unhooked.com/sep/index.htm
Reading list with links to many articles.

Recommended Reading – Books and Articles

Barrett, Clarence, JD. *Beyond AA: Dealing Responsibly with Alcohol.* Greenleaf, OR: Positive Attitudes, 1991.

Browne, Gerald J. *Treatment Doesn't Work.* Scotia, New York: Baldwin Research   Institute, Inc., p. 16-34, 1991. (See www.baldwinresearch.com for other articles and links)

Bufe, Charles. *Alcoholics Anonymous: Cult or Cure?* San Francisco: See Sharp Press,   1991.

Bufe, Charles, Peele, Stanton, Brodsky, Archie, and Horvath, Thomas (Introduction).   *Resisting 12-step Coercion: How to Fight Forced Participation in AA, NA, or 12- step Treatment.* Tuscon, AZ: See Sharp Press, 2000.

Burton, Kathleen, Schuerger, James M. Ph.D., Santoro, David A., Ph.D., Lonsdale, Derrick, MD, *A Placebo Controlled Study of the Supplementary Effects of Thiamin Tetrahydrofuryl Disulfide (TTFD) in Recovering Chemically Addicted Individuals.* Journal of Advancement in Medicine, Volume 6, November 3, Fall 1993.

Christopher, James. *Unhooked: Staying Sober and Drug-free.* Buffalo: Prometheus   Books, 1989.

_____. *SOS Sobriety: The Proven Alternative to 12-step Programs.* Buffalo: Prometheus Books, 1992.

Claiborn, James, Ph.D. & Pedrick, Cherry, R.N. *The Habit Change Workbook.* New York: New Harbinger Publications, Inc., 2001.

Daley, Dennis C. *Kicking Addictive Habits Once and for All.* San Francisco, OH: Jossey-   Bass Inc., Publishers, 1991.

DeLuca, Alexander F., M.D. *Abstinence vs. Harm Reduction: a False Dichotomy.* www.doctordeluca.com/library, August, 2000.

DeSena, James, Schaler, Jeffrey A. & Gerstein, Joseph. *Overcoming YourAlcohol, Drug and Recovery Habits.* Tuscon, AZ: See Sharp Press, 2003.

Dodes, Lance M. *The Heart of Addiction.* New York: HarperCollins Publishers, 2002.

Dorsman, Jerry. *How to Quit Drinking Without AA.* Tuscon, NY: Three Rivers Press, 1997.

Ellis, Albert, & Velton, Emmett, Ph.D. *When AA Doesn't Work For You*. New York: New Harbinger Publications, Inc., 2002.

Fletcher, A.M. *Sober for Good*. Boston: Houghton Mifflin, 2001.

Galanter, Marc, MD; Egelko, Susan, Ph.D., and Edwards, Helen, MPH. "Rational Recovery: Alternative to AA for Addiction," *American Journal of Drug & Alcohol Abuse:* 19 (4), pp. 499-510 (1993).

Glatt, M.M. *Controlled Drinking After A Third Of A Century: Comments on Sobell & Sobell*. Addiction, 90, 1157-1160, 1995.

Hackl, John R., and Hackl, Alphons J. *The Way Out of Alcoholism*. Washington, DC: Acropolis Books, 1984.

Heather, N. *The great controlled drinking consensus: Is it premature?:* Addiction, 90, 1160-1162, 1995.

Hersey, Brook, Psy.M. *The Controlled Drinking Debates: A Review of Four Decades of Acrimony*. www.doctordeluca.com/library, April, 2001.

Kirkpatrick, Jean, Ph.D. *Goodbye Hangovers, Hello Life*. New York: Atheneum, 1986.

Kishline, A. *Moderate Drinking: The Moderation Management Guide For People Who Want To Reduce Their Drinking*. New York: Crown, 1994.

Lemanski, Michael J. *Addiction Alternatives for Recovery*. *Gale Group*, 2000. www.findarticles.com.

Markert, Louis F., Ph.D. & Nikakhtar, Manijeh, MD. *Addiction or Self Medication? The Truth*. New York: Barricfade Books, 1992.

Marlatt, G.A. *Research and Political Realities: What the Next Twenty Years Hold For Behaviorists in the Alcohol Field*. Advances in Behavior Research and Therapy, 9, 165-171, 1987.

Marx, Jack. *Now That the Party's Over*. The Sydney Morning Herald, January 1, 2005. (See website for article and links to others)
http://radar.smh.com.au/archives/2005/01/now that the pa.htm

1.)

Mathews-Larsen, Joan, Ph.D. *Alcoholism, The Biochemical Connection: A Breakthrough Seven-Week Self-Treatment Program.* New York: Villard Books, 1992.

Milam, Dr. James R., and Ketcham, Katherine. *Under the Influence: A Guide to the Myths and Realities of Alcoholism.* Seattle: Madrona Publishers, 1981.

Ogilvie, Heather. *Alternatives to Abstinence.* New York: Hatherleigh Press, 2001.

Peele, Stanton. *Cures depend on attitudes, not programs.* Los Angeles Times, March 14, 1990. (See www.peele.net/lib/index.html for numerous articles.)

Peele, Stanton. *The Meaning of Addiction.* Boston: Lexington Books, 1985.

Peele, Stanton, and Brodsky, Archie, with Arnold, Mary. *The Truth About Addiction and Recovery: The Life Process Program for Outgrowing Destructive Habits.* New York: Simon & Schuster, 1991.

Plagenhoef, Richard L., MD, and Adler, Carol. *Why Am I Still Addicted?: A holistic Approach to Recovery.* Blue Ridge Summit, PA: Tab Books, 1992.

Ragge, Ken. *The Real AA: The Myth Behind Twelve Step Recovery.* Tuscon, AZ: See Sharp Press, 1998.

Rotgers, Frederick, Kern, Marc & Hoeltzel, Rudy. *Responsible Drinking: A Moderation Management Approach For Problem Drinkers.* Oakland, CA: New Harbinger, 2002.

Sanchez-Craig, M., Annis, H.M., Bornet, A.R. & MacDonald, K.R. Random Assignment to Abstinence and Controlled Drinking: Evaluation of a Cognitive-Behavioral Program for Problem Drinkers. Journal Of Consulting and Clinical Psychology, 52, 390-403, 1984.

Schaler, Jeffrey A., Ph.D. *Addiction As A Choice.* Peru, IL: Open court Publishing Company, 2000.

Sobell, M.B. & Sobell, L.C. Alcoholics Treated by Individualized Behavior Therapy: One Year Treatment Outcomes. Behavior Research and Therapy, 11, 599-618, 1973.

Sobell, M.B. & Sobell, L.C. Controlled Drinking After 25 Years: How Important Was the Great Debate? Addiction, 90, 1149-1153, 1995.

Szalavitz, Maia. *Breaking Out of the 12-step Lockstep.* Washington Post. pB03, June 9th, 2002.

Trimpey, Jack. *The Small Book: A Revolutionary Alternative for Overcoming Alcohol and Drug Dependence.* New York: Delacorte, 1992.

Trimpey, Jack. *Rational Recovery: The New Cure for Substance Addiction.* New York: Pocket Books, 1996.

Trimpey, Jack. *The American "Treatment" Tragedy.* Lotus Press, 1994.

Valliant, George E. *The Natural History of Alcoholism, Revisited.* Cambridge, MA: Harvard University Press, 1993.

Volpicelli, Joseph & Szalavitz, Maia. *Recovery Options.* New York: John Wiley & Sons, Inc., 1994.

White, W.L. *Slaying The Dragon: The History of Addiction Treatment and Recovery in America.* Bloomington, IL: Chestnut Health Systems, 1998.

Winters, Ariel. *Alternatives for the Problem Drinker: AA Is Not the Only Way.* New York: Drake Publishers, 1978.

Notes

Introduction:

1. Brown, Gerald J. *Treatment Doesn't Work.* Scotia, New York: Baldwin Research Institute, Inc., pgs 16-34, 1991.

2. (No author listed) *Comments on AA's Triennial Surveys.* New York: Alcoholics Anonymous World Services, Inc.

3. Kolenda, Richard, *"Analysis of Comments on AA's Triennial Surveys",* Golden Text Publishing, pgs 1-2, 2003

4. Alcoholics Anonymous World Services. *Alcoholics Anonymous Big Book, 4th Edition.* New York: Alcoholics Anonymous World Services, Inc. Chapter 5, p.58.

5. Vacovsky, Lloyd. *Finding Effective Treatment for Alcohol Dependence.* American Council on Alcoholism, May 12, 2005.

6. Wilson, William. *AA Comes of Age.* New York: Alcoholics Anonymous World Services, p.232.

7. *Treatment of Drug Abuse and Addiction- Part III.* The Harvard Mental Health Letter, Volume 12, Number 4, October 1995, page 3.

8. Sobell, Mark, and Sobell Linda. *Behavioral Treatment of Alcohol Problems.* New York: Plenum Press, 1978, p.166.

Section I

Part One:

1. SOS information, from SOS website: www.secularsobriety.org.

2. SMART information, from SMART website: www.smartrecovery.org.

3. LifeRing information, from website: www.unhooked.com.

4. Rational Recovery information, from RR website: www.rational.org.

5. Menzies, Percy. *Why is recovery fro Alcoholism so difficult? And is there hope for successful treatment?* American council on Alcoholism, May 12, 2005.

6. Pennsylvania Model Information, from Assisted Recovery Centers of

America website: www.assistedrecovery.com.

Part Two:

1. Women for Sobriety Information, from WFS website:
   www.womenforsobriety.org.

2. Kasl, Charlotte, M.D. *16-Steps for Discovery and Empowerment.*
   www.charlottekasl.com/16steps.html

3. Kasl, Charlotte, M.D. *Zen, Feminism, and Recovery: 16 Steps for Discovery and Empowerment.* www.addictioninfo.org/content/articles, February 5, 2005.

Part Three:

1. Moderation Management Information, from MM website:
   www.moderation.org

2. Sinclair Method Information from Sinclair website:
   www.sinclairmethod.com and www.newerahealthcenter.com.

3. Denning, Patt, Little, Jeannie, Glickman, Adina, *Over the Influence The Harm Reduction Guide for Managing Drugs and Alcohol.* New York: The Guilford Press, p.3, 2004.

Section II:
1. Prentiss, Chris, *The Alcoholism and Addiction Cure A Holistic Approach to Total Recovery.* Los Angeles: Power Press, p.242, 211-212, 2006.

Section IV:
1. Hester, R.K., Miller, W.R. *Handbook of Alcoholism Treatment Approaches: Effective Alternatives* (3rd Edition). Boston: Allyn & Bacon, 2003, Chapter 2.

Section VI:

1. Trimpey, Jack. *AA: America's State Religion?* Excerpted from Rational Recovery Political and Legal Action Network, http://members.purespeed.com/~mg/Alcoholics_Anonymous.html.
2. Peele, Stanton, Ph.D., J.D. *Is AA's loss psychology's gain?* Monitor on Psychology, Volume 35, No. 7 July/August 2004, p.86.

Conclusion:

1. Addiction Resource Center, Inc. Information at website: www.arcinc.org

About Melanie Solomon

After a twelve-year battle with addiction, including a vicious cycle of rehabs, sober livings, 12-step meetings, recovery, relapse, and overdosing, Melanie Solomon is now living a normal, balanced, functioning life.

A full-time writer and lecturer, Ms. Solomon has taught at the Huntington Beach School District's Drug and Alcohol Program and has spoken at The Learning Annex in California. She graduated from the U. of Michigan, with a B.A. in psychology with honors. While making Phi Beta Kappa, she also volunteered at the school's Women's Center, counseling and placing abused and/or chemically addicted women into safe facilities.

She had to drop out of UCLA Law School after completing one year to enter a well-known, conventional rehab, which is where she was first introduced to AA and the 12-steps. This began the 12 year odyssey of addiction & treatment that concluded with an experience that left her for nearly dead on several occassions.

It was then that she realized that there had to be another way. Due to her unyielding research of alternatives to AA, and the other 12-step programs, she started uncovering the scientific research that had been going on for over 3 decades, which sadly, most Americans are largely unaware of, such as according to AA's own internal surveys covering a 5-year period, as well as numerous government and independent studies, AA had only a 3-5% success rate for those who even stuck around for a year, and that 93-97% of the treatment centers in the US are still 12-step based! Even though there are many viable, evidence-based alternatives, well accepted and established in other countries, that might better suit the complex and individualized needs of people suffering with substance abuse problems.

She now devotes her life to researching recovery options, and then sharing these findings with others. First through her book, and now through her website, where there is a wealth of information about alternatives, current research, and other products, as well as a FREE discussion room, open to those in need themselves, loved ones, or professionals in the field, which will expand the dialog & knowledge about recovery options.

Besides being a full time author, Ms. Solomon now works for Outskirts Press, Inc., a publishing company, where she works with authors to help them market their books.

If you are interested in interviewing Ms. Solomon, or having her speak to your group, contact her through her website, www.aanottheonlyway.com, by email, aanottheonlyway@gmail.com, or directly at 310-658-0990.

Do you know of others who would benefit from AA – Not the Only Way?

You can order online at www.AANotTheOnlyWay.com, or by calling 310-658-0990. Quantity discounts available. For treatment programs & other institutions, may now order in bulk boxes of 25, 50 or 100 for their clients, either as part of their treatment or discharge plan, or to use for professional, educational workshops or seminars. Call author for full details.

Join Our Support Community

If you are interested in an ongoing dialog with others that are trying to get a grip on their chemical dependencies, go to AANotTheOnlyWay.com and join our forum.

Join our E-Mail List

Do you want to stay informed about the latest 12 step alternatives? Then go to www.AANotTheOnlyWay.com and join our mailing list.

Are You Aware Of A Treatment Program That Is Not In The Book?

There are constant discoveries and innovations being developed to help in the area of chemical dependency treatment programs. Please let us know of anything that would be beneficial for future updates of AA-Not The Only Way.

Send submissions to: aanottheonlyway@gmail.com

Do You Need One-On-One Coaching?

Melanie Solomon has a wealth of wisdom to help you achieve your life goals. If you need help overcoming your chemical dependencies, or you just want to achieve a higher level of success.

Coaching – Try A Free Session

Getting coaching is easy. Take the first step. Start with a FREE sample session.
Baskin Robbins gives out complimentary tastes of their ice cream, I offer coaching sessions. These samples give you an experiential "taste" of future results. What we do is spend 20 to 30 minutes on the telephone, or in person, to discuss your goals, intentions, and aspirations, and it gives you the experience of being coached.

What do you talk about during the session. Start with your vision your dreams, and the outcomes you are trying to achieve. Or talk about your greatest challenges, and how to overcome them. By the end of the free sample session you will be in action. You will have a sense of our potential partnership as coach and client, a better vision of your goals, and a plan to achieve them. You will move from trying to doing.

To schedule a free session, dial 310-658-0990, or go to my website, www.aanottheonlyway.com and sign up there.